CONCILIUM

Religion in the Eighties

CONCILIUM

Editorial Directors

Concilium 173 (3/1984): Sociology of Religion

CONCILIUM

List of Members

Advisory Committee: Sociology of Religion

THE SEXUAL REVOLUTION

Edited by
Gregory Baum
John Coleman

English Language Editor
Marcus Lefébure

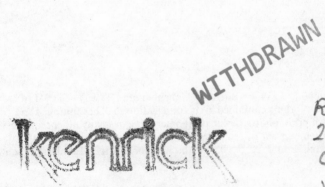
T. & T. CLARK LTD
Edinburgh

June 1984
T. & T. Clark Ltd, 36 George Street, Edinburgh EH2 2LQ
ISBN: 0 567 30053 6

ISSN: 0010-5236

Typeset by C. R. Barber & Partners (Highlands) Ltd, Fort William
Printed in Scotland by Blackwood, Pillans & Wilson Ltd, Edinburgh

Concilium: Published February, April, June, August, October, December.
Subscriptions 1984: USA: US$40.00 (including air mail postage and packing); Canada:
Canadian$50.00 (including air mail postage and packing); UK and rest of the world:
£19.00 (including postage and packing).

CONTENTS

Part III
Christian Reactions

Editorial

THE RAPID change of sexual mores in the industrialised capitalist countries of the West is often referred to as 'the sexual revolution'. Sociologists have examined the phenomenon in detail. In countries or regions that have been industrialised for a long time the change has been a gradual one, though speeding up in the last decades, while in countries or regions in which industrialisation and the accompanying 'modernization' have been introduced more recently, the change has been sudden and startling. The new phenomenon demands reflection by the moral philosopher. More than that it demands critical Christian reflection and an appropriate pastoral response on the part of the Christian Churches. Because the new phenomenon is complex and open to diverging interpretations, it is important to submit it to a careful examination before attempting to offer a Christian reaction. In this issue of *Concilium* we wish to study the sexual revolution, its interpretations and its accompanying social effects and then take a brief look at the Catholic responses. The point we wish to make is that Christian reflection on sexual conduct is valid and truthful only if the empirical human reality has been carefully examined. There is no methodological shortcut. Only after we have analysed the new phenomenon can we search for the meaning of the Gospel in regard to human sexuality today.

In the first section of this issue it was our intention to study the empirical phenomenon of the sexual revolution. Since the description of social reality is never totally distinct from our interpretation of it, the first section also looks at certain interpretative frameworks that have been offered. The first article by Fourez offers an historical perspective which reveals that sexual mores are to a large extent related to the organisation of society. Then follow two case studies, by Gagnon and Acquaviva, that examine the sexual revolution in the USA and Italy respectively. While Gagnon pursues a scientific, value-free approach, Acquavivà introduces some ethical reflections. He is concerned because the new sexual mores in Italy are not associated with any particular societal project. The final article of this section, by Siebert, analyses the Frankfurt School interpretation of the sexual revolution.

Very often the rapid change of sexual mores is seen in one or two ideological frameworks, the first one 'liberal' and the second 'conservative'. The liberal perspective offers an evolutionary interpretation of society's entry into modernity. The passage from *Gemeinschaft* to *Gesellschaft*, from folk to urban society, is here regarded as progress. Here an ever greater emergence of personal freedom and personal autonomy has overcome and left behind the religious, moral and social bonds that made traditional society a closely woven community of shared values. Here the recent sexual liberation appears as the victory of the autonomous self capable of assuming full responsibility for his or her sexual behaviour in the quest for greater personal fulfilment. The conservative perspective, on the other hand, regards the sexual revolution in wholly negative terms: it sees it as the decline of virtue, the rejection of moral and religious authority, and the emergence of selfishness with devastating consequences for society as a whole. The sexual revolution must be resisted: there is nothing we can learn from it. In this issue of *Concilium* neither one nor the other perspective is represented, every author recognises the enormous ambiguity of the new phenomenon. Most of the authors recognise on the one hand the value of freedom, that is a person's call to have a free, nonrepressive, responsible and fully human relationship to his or her sexuality; and they recognise on the other hand the social meaning of sexuality and hence the dangers to society created by the universal pursuit of personal fulfilment. Fourez, at least, questions the new individualism that threatens to undermine the social project. Siebert who represents the neo-Marxist approach of the Frankfurt School comes to conclusions, on a radical basis, that do not differ much from traditional Western values, religious and secular. Siebert even believes that this neo-Marxist philosophy, because of its trust in utopia of justice, described only *via negativa*, remains open to the supernatural. Acquaviva tells us that in Italy the sexual revolution promoted by the consumers' society and hedonistic capitalism greatly disturbs both Catholic and Marxist leaders.

It would have been important to have another article in this context that brought out the positive elements of the sexual revolution, namely the overcoming of self-damaging repression and access to greater personal integration. According to Freud at least, repression is destructive. The return of repressed sexuality nourishes the power drive, distorts the perception of reality, and easily fosters domination over other people.

Overcoming repression leads to a new, more creative self-possession. In his book, *Leonardo da Vinci*, Freud even holds out the hope that the overcoming of repression may liberate, through a psychic process called sublimation, libidinal energy in the service of cultural and spiritual creativity. Because the editors did not know what positions the authors of this issue would adopt in their articles, this issue lacks an article that clarifies the positive aspects of the sexual revolution.

Section two deals with some of the social consequences of the sexual revolution. In her article, 'The Sexual Revolution and Violence Against Women', Hanks shows that while the sexual revolution affirms the freedom and equality of each person and hence intends to promote mutuality and respect, in actual fact there is evidence that the age old violence exercised by men against women in rape, battering, incest, and pornography is by no means being overcome. The call for sexual liberation may simply disguise new efforts to dominate women and actually harm them. What has changed, however, is this: while in the past male violence against women was not publicly acknowledged, it was in fact often protected by the law, the sad facts are today revealed by the women's movement. Society is made to see the widespread violence against women. While the women's movement welcomes the sexual revolution inasmuch as it promotes freedom and mutuality it vehemently opposes many aspects of the new permissive society. Women fight against pornography, and they demand laws and social institutions that offer protection to women who suffer violence from the men in their own families.

Hortelano examines the difficulties created for the family by the rapid change of sexual mores. Despite the threat to family stability, he does not take a wholly negative view: he proposes a new pastoral approach to married life that summons couples to greater friendship and reciprocity in their relationships.

The new conditions created in highly industrialised countries of the West allow homosexual men and women, for the first time in history, to acknowledge their sexual orientation in public, to create their own social organisations, and to produce reflections and studies based on their own experiences. In his article Coleman argues that we have today, for the first time, a homosexual discourse. Both the social scientist and the moralist have available to them, in documents and institutions, the self-understanding of homosexual men and women. There exists a growing literature in which homosexuals reflect on the ethical, social, political and religious implications of their human existence. Coleman argues that the moral philosopher and the Christian theologian in their evaluation of homosexuality must take into account the existing homosexual discourse. Coleman does not suggest what conclusions Christian moral theology should come to. His point is that no judgment on homosexuality whether by social scientists or moralists, has validity if it has not taken seriously dialogue with the self-understanding of gay people.

Is there a relation between the rebelliousness of youth and the new sexual mores? Lazure argues that in the countries where youth was highly publicised in the sixties, researchers find that more recently youth has retreated from politics. To what extent do they remain critics of society? And what are the implications for their sexual mores? Is there a return to a more conservative moral stance?

The editors of this issue intended to publish an article in this section that would deal with the disruption of traditional societies, especially in the Third World, caused by tourism and other forms of cultural and commercial invasions of the West. In many parts of the world, religious leaders, including bishops of the Christian churches, have raised their voices in protest against the devastating impact of the new mores on their people. Unfortunately we had to go to press without the appropriate article.

Section three of this issue deals very briefly with the Christian responses to the sexual revolution. We confine ourselves to the Catholic reactions. Among the Protestant Churches there is a much wider spectrum of theological evaluation and moral guidelines. The Decree on Ecumenism, promulgated by Vatican Council II, demands that Catholic moral theologians engage in dialogue with their Protestant colleagues, and even if they come to different conclusions Catholics must remember that their Protestant brothers and sisters are inspired by the same intention to remain faithful to Christ. It would have been interesting to examine the wide divergence among the responses of the Christian Churches. To what extent are these differences determined by cultural and historical factors? Yet we had no space for such an investigation.

Of great importance is the 1976 Vatican Declaration on Sexual Matters which wants to correct the tendency to permissiveness found among some Catholic theologians. It is a conservative statement intent upon protecting the inherited norms. The article by Grecco presents a careful analysis of Pope John Paul II's sermons on human sexuality, which introduce a new approach in the Church's official teaching. The phenomenological approach pursued by John Paul II leads to a perception of human sexuality that focuses on subjectivity and recognises the central part it plays in the creation of personal self-identity. John Paul II's philosophical and theological reflections introduce a new theme in the Church's *magisterium*. Yet his phenomenological method overlooks the sociological dimension of people's self-understanding as did traditional ecclesiastical teaching based on an essentially unchanging natural law. Thévenot's article deals with theology's critical dialogue with modern society and its sexual mores. He regards the contemporary approach to sexuality in its full ambiguity. Christian theology will have to integrate certain aspects of this modern, more liberal self-understanding, and at the same time it offers a prophetic challenge to other aspects of the sexual revolution. Like most of the authors in this collection Thévenot is especially sensitive to the social dimension of human sexuality, and hence he regrets both the individualism implicit in the sexual revolution and the objectification of sexuality as commodity in the seryice of capitalist economy. Andolsen offers the reader a report from the USA recording the widespread dissent of dedicated Catholics in matters of sexual behaviour. The critical reflections of these Catholics based on their own spiritual experiences, while having no place in official Church teaching, finds support in the writings of some Christian theologians, especially Protestant, with a significant number of Catholics among them. These Catholics believe that the Catholic Church which has moved so much in its official teaching since Vatican II, especially in recognising sexuality as a dimension of the human person and in accepting the moral concept of responsible parenthood, will eventually modify its present position. At this time the 1976 Vatican Declaration on Sexual Matters remains normative in the Church.

GREGORY BAUM
JOHN COLEMAN

PART I

The New Phenomenon

Gérard Fourez

The Sexual Revolution in Perspective

ALTHOUGH IT is obvious that the idea of 'sexual revolution' has an empirical reference, it is still difficult to define. It has also to be situated within a context that will help to explain its causes and development and the issues at stake. My aim in writing this article is to show how the sexual revolution and the ethics of affective life, the body and sexuality are socially conditioned. This analysis will obviously be a simplified theoretical and therefore also ideological construction and will incorporate within a single representation several historical developments that differ from each other according to period, place, culture, social class and sex. Many aspects of the problem will inevitably be neglected in my study and my approach to these contemporary questions will also be my own. One of my central presuppositions is that there is no universal analysis of these phenomena.[1]

1. THE BODY OF AUTARKIC SOCIETIES IN THE MIDDLE AGES

During the feudal period, before the rise of the bourgeoisie, economic organisation was fairly autarkic. The domains—rural villas, castles and monasteries—and villages which were connected with it produced a considerable number of their own consumer goods and tools. What we have since come to call the differentiation of roles was very little known in those communities. When someone needed shoes, he did not go to the shoemaker, but to Ernest or Anatole, who made shoes. Relationships were, in other words, not primarily functional, but essentially personal and global. The inhabitants of these communities knew each other well and that knowledge went beyond the functional relationships that united them. Work was not so much a specialised activity as a sharing in the global structure.

Economic, political and social realities were not separate then as they are now. People could not think of themselves as existing outside their own community and exile was worse than death. In these groups—and they exist now to some extent in certain traditional communities and groups of young people—everyone knew everyone else globally. To some degree it is possible to say that everyone knew the 'body' of the others in the community. There were clear and sacralised prohibitions with regard to the body, but one has the impression that the problem of modesty did not exist in the same way as it exists now. People slept together in inns, for example, without the same moral problems that this would undoubtedly have caused for our grandparents. Several of the bye-laws of the city

3

of Paris that have survived from the middle ages to the present day are typical in this regard.

A good example is the practice of nude bathing in the River Seine. It is possible to observe from a study of the increasingly strict Parisian bye-laws a gradual change in social customs. The same progress can also be detected in sea-side bathing. The final stage in this development was reached at the beginning of the present century. It strikes us now as laughable, but at that time bathers were taken almost fully dressed in their cabins to the water's edge and they entered the sea with their bodies being hardly seen.

If we are to understand the idea of the body in the middle ages, we should remember that capital hardly existed at that time. The surplus of production was not invested with growth in mind. It was generally used in sumptuary spending on feasts, wars or cathedrals, for example. This attitude is reflected in the medieval idea of the body. On the one hand, it was regarded as the working body which obtained what was required to sustain life in the present and throughout the following season. (It did not, however, ever come to be regarded simply as a tool.) On the other hand, it was also seen at certain times as the feasting body. (One has only to think in this regard of the rather later paintings of Bruegel or of other situations that we, with our thrifty middle-class attitudes, call 'excesses'.) In the aristocratic classes, this feasting body was revealed in prestige spending on tournaments and wars. All this is far removed from the parsimonious nineteenth century with its questions about whether excesses of this kind were not too tiring, with a damaging effect on health and work.

The morality of this period reflects the organisation of society. In other words, it formed a single whole. Norms appealed more to the 'sacred' than to the 'rational'. Bodies, social distinctions, sexual differences and so on were attributed to that 'sacred' sphere that had been given by God.[2] A transgression was not primarily seen as turning a means away from its end. It was rather regarded as affecting the whole of the social and even the cosmic order. Morality consisted of sacred prohibitions and was intimately connected with shame rather than with blame. Ethical thinking stressed harmony with nature and the virtues that came from this. It was not until the fourteenth century and William of Ockham that morality began to be taught in negative precepts. Later still, the authors of manuals of moral theology began to approach sexuality as something that had to be controlled in the perspective of a criterion of 'yield', in other words, of procreation. Reason was the factor that indicated what could or could not be done according to the measure of these objectives.

2. BOURGEOIS BODIES

At the end of the middle ages, there was a marked cultural change. This change can be understood if we look at the model of the bourgeois merchant going from one town to another in Europe and establishing regular trade relationships with his customers not on a global basis, but by means of contracts. What is more, the merchant thought of himself as alone, in a state of 'inner exile'.[3] An individualistic conception of man and morality originated with the merchant, who made so many journeys away from his home that a clear distinction came about between his private life and his public, professional life. He found his roots in his inner life as something distinct from his constantly changing external activity. As time passed, that distinction became apparent in architectural design—houses became 'interiors' (and were soon locked), bedrooms were clearly distinguished from the rooms where business took place and monastic enclosures were strengthened. The division between masculine and feminine rôles became wider and women were treated, much more emphatically than they had hitherto been, as minors.[4]

The phenomenon of the division of labour appeared and the professions became so differentiated that it is possible for us now to do business with someone when we know only his functions and nothing about his private life. The economic surplus was no longer spent on feasts, but frugally preserved as capital. The bourgeois attitude was above all thrifty and rational and concentrated on efficiency and what produced a return from investment. The aristocracy continued for centuries to live in accordance with the earlier way of thinking and behaving, but did not come into conflict with the bourgeoisie. In the well-known fable of the grasshopper and the ant, the former is the aristocrat who does not acquire money and the latter is the bourgeois, the thrifty merchant. Deliberate self-control became the main virtue of bourgeois ethics. The foundations of a new and very 'masculine' morality, based on 'love and self-control' were laid.

Man's understanding of the body altered with these socio-economic changes. The bourgeois merchant once again provides us with a model. In the external sphere of his life, his body lost all affective meaning. He came to be regarded as a means, a tool or even—we have only to think of Descartes—as a machine or an automaton. His affective existence gradually retreated into a new inner sphere—that of his private life. The family was presented more and more as a very small group consisting of relations and children—the nuclear family. Bourgeois ethics led to the practice of keeping the body at a distance—people did not eat from the same dishes or drink from the same cup and touched each other much less. In towns and cities, individuals lived side by side without ever knowing one another and it was not long before they ceased to speak to each other. Moral norms similarly became inner principles rather than prohibitions. Feelings retreated into the 'inner life' and this led to the appearance of romantic love. The rest of social life was governed by business considerations. Religion came to place more and more emphasis on the spiritual life, which was increasingly identified with the inner life. At the same time, interiority and the mystical or scientific knowledge associated with it became the motivating force of bourgeois society.

An ethic of calculation and of saving became the basis of the new morality of the body and of affective or sexual life. The bourgeoisie did not see sexuality as part of the global nature of the world giving everything its place. It was rather an object of reflection linked to the increasingly great value accorded to the individual. One had to control oneself in order to 'realise' oneself. The central problem of the bourgeois ethic was how to control one's passions, since these had such irrational power that they threatened the calculations to which everything was subordinate.

From the eighteenth century onwards, the bourgeoisie was above all concerned with the management of the passions as it was with the management of affairs. People looked increasingly for a morality of calculation and teachers and physicians who could teach them how to control their bodies and therefore be more open to reason. Their ideal was to make instruments of them—strong, healthy, calm, sober, well ordered tools that could be used for work or procreation. But man's affective nature cannot be fitted so easily into such rational patterns, with the result that systems of sexual repression were developed in the eighteenth and nineteenth centuries. The bourgeois morality of marriage also reflects the economic order and seems to be based on the private property of the husband and wife, that is, the ownership of one by the other or at least of the wife by the husband. According to M. Foucault, it is only then that the concept of 'sexuality' is structured separately from a more global perspective in order to describe, within a complex of technical arguments, what has to be controlled and brought within the framework of norms devised for this purpose.[5] This 'bourgeois' morality is not what the apostles of the sexual revolution sometimes claim that it is, a stupid and scrupulous form of repression. It is rather a massive affirmation of the individual and his strength. It is important, then to know how the (male?) individual and his sexuality fit into the world that the bourgeoisie aimed to build up.

B

3. FROM INDIVIDUALISM TO THE INDUSTRIAL REVOLUTION

As the bourgeoisie became the dominant class in society, it began to undermine the earlier aristocratic ethic and at the same the sacral morality of the people. The individual, who was now conducting his affairs independently of royal power, became bold enough to assert himself and his own life-style. This individualism reached a peak in the eighteenth century. The United States Declaration of Independence is perhaps the most striking evidence of this in its affirmation that every human being has the right to pursue his happiness. This little sentence is extremely subversive with regard to the old order, in which the individual had a place only in the sacred organisation of society. (It should not be forgotten that it was almost impossible for the individual to think of himself as alone in the earlier autarkic form of society.)

This right to pursue one's own happiness was a direct result of liberal individualism, but it was also to undermine the bourgeois society that had produced it. When all other conditions had been fulfilled, the policy of preserving one's inheritance and of calculating a 'yield' was abandoned in favour of marrying 'for love' or, at a later stage, of achieving 'success' in one's affective life.

Man's understanding of his body and his private life was further changed when trade-guilds disappeared and industrial society developed. This change was above all promoted by the growth of the (individual) employment market and the increasing separation between the place of work and the place of abode. Throughout the nineteenth and twentieth centuries, most family workshops and even family businesses were replaced by more impersonal places of work, where life was regulated by reason and increasingly by technology. In these places, the workers came to experience their bodies in a new way and they were followed in the twentieth century by management and executive staff. The body was felt as alienated and something over which one had, in the world of work, less and less control.

Private life was, however, greatly strengthened by the appearance of this world of work. Human existence became divided into two spheres: the private sphere, centred on the nuclear family and the place of abode and the public sphere of work and social interactivity. The latter is theoretically 'asexual', in that only technological and economic rationality, in other words, bourgeois rationality, was within the state. The whole of affective life is confined to the former.

With increasing local mobility, the family system continues to change. The family is now reduced to its basic form of a cell and has lost many of its most important functions. Adults work away from home in the factory and similarly children are for the most part educated at school. The mobility of labour has led to the function of 'social security' being transferred to public organisations, with a consequent weakening of traditional solidarity. The family is left with the task of being a place of affectivity and a cell of consumerism. The married couple are liberated from certain social functions, but a great deal is still demanded of them—lacking the extended family, they have great difficulty in ensuring the affective security of their children. Living in a society with frequent changes of address, moreover, the husband and wife are the only stable affective relationship for each other. This is a very heavy burden to bear and it is made heavier by a new moral norm (connected with the right to pursue individual happiness): 'you must achieve success in your affective life'. The more that is expected of the married couple, the more difficult this 'success' is. And, as always in such cases, the threatened institution is given an ideological value. Family groups and movements, home sharing and marriage encounters have, for example, come into being in Christian circles. Giving a high value to affectivity and creating a spirituality of affective life are the first signs of the sexual revolution.

4. THE REVOLT OF EROS AGAINST LOGOS

During the period of industrialisation, it was always the bourgeois morality with its aim of controlling self and the world that made itself felt. Towards the end of the nineteenth century, however, sexuality, which had been repressed everywhere, began to reassert itself. The analyses of Freud, who was undoubtedly one of the last bourgeois moralists, and Marcuse, the philosopher of the cultural revolution of the nineteen-sixties, are of great significance in this context.

Freud, it is well known, protested against the repression of sexuality, but he was also anxious about sexual urges.[6] He wondered whether modern man, subjected to the logic of industrial society, would be able to go on paying the price of civilisation, which was, he believed, the control of his urges. He believed that the principles of reality and reason had to subjugate the spontaneity of those urges, in other words, that Logos had to dominate Eros. He was afraid that the whole structure of civilisation might collapse without that repression. In that respect, he was certainly at one with his period. His work can be interpreted as a last (?) attempt on the part of bourgeois civilisation to control sexuality by directing the urges. The strategy that he suggested differed from that of bourgeois society, but his intention remained essentially bourgeois—the management of the libido. Spontaneity had to be mistrusted. It had to be directed and sublimated. The question is highly characteristic of bourgeois culture: How can the individual assert himself without being overcome by the irrationality of his urges?

Marcuse also believed that our civilisation had been built on the repression of spontaneity in order to let reason dominate. In his opinion, however, the prosperous society produced by economic success, itself the result of sexual repression, had deprived that very repression of its usefulness. Logos continued, however, to dominate Eros because the bourgeoisie had replaced the principle of reality with that of yield. Marcuse called this over-repression. In his opinion, we produce more not in order to meet our needs as defined by reality, but rather in order to maintain economic growth and obtain a yield from it. This process is subjected to the cool rationality—which is historically masculine—of the technologies that now dominate us. Because of this, Eros continues to be subjected to Logos, but now the subjection is irrational. That, Marcuse believed, is the cause of the sexual revolution—the final revolt of Eros, spontaneity, against Logos.

5. THE SEXUAL REVOLUTION AND THE MIDDLE CLASSES

The sexual revolution of the mid-twentieth century seems to have begun in the upper middle classes. These are characterised—or can be defined—by their ambiguous relationship with power. They do not have the impression that they are influencing events, since capital and political class are decisive there, but they enjoy sufficient economic, financial and cultural privileges to want to maintain the social system. There can therefore only be a revolution in the private lives of members of this class. They work hard, pay high taxes, cannot expect to move higher in society and often find their work disappointing. They would therefore seem to form the ideal class for Marcusian over-repression. (These analyses would have to be differentiated in terms of the masculine and the feminine to indicate how female emancipation and revolt have played a part in the sexual revolution.)

Before it became merged with the middle classes, the aristocracy had a pre-bourgeois morality. Like the bourgeoisie, the urban and rural working classes[7] have also never had the impression that they are in control of their lives and this also applies to the women of those classes.[8] They leave the norms of bourgeois morality to those who have a place in society and try above all to manage as well as they can and to combine the theoretical affirmation of a strict and sacral morality with a more tolerant praxis. For a long time, working classes and the rising social classes were very suspicious of the permissiveness of the 'liberal' or 'liberated' morality of the privileged classes. In Europe, for example, the working class is more prudish than the upper middle class and, in the United States, the 'moral majority' express the ordinary people's hesitation to follow the 'élites'. For some fifteen years, however, the sexual revolution—and/or the ideology of the middle classes?—has had an impact on the young members of almost every social class in Western society.

This brief analysis of the situation of the middle classes should enable us to understand one of the characteristic elements of the sexual revolution—the withdrawal into the private, affective, family and sexual sphere. This movement can be summed up in the image of the little house or flat in which the nuclear family lives, withdrawn into itself. At work and in the commuter-work-home-to-bed syndrome, the middle-class person today has hardly any control over his life, so he tries to find some by experimenting in his private, affective, family and sexual life. But, in our producer-consumer society, this kind of experiment often remains at the level of the audio-visual, with the result that there is hardly any change in his basic repressions.

Seen in this perspective, the sexual revolution forms part of an immense movement of 'privatisation' in human existence, highly characteristic of advanced industrial and technological society. Those who have given up believing that it is worth investing in the public sphere or in achieving greater socio-political power invest in affective and sexual experience, sensitivity and other training groups and even in religious affectivity. Generally speaking, then, we can accept that the sexual revolution is the result of an attempt to rediscover control over one's life—unable to achieve it in the public sphere, people are looking for it in their private and family lives. Finally, the 'sexual revolution' is an integrating element in industrial society, producing new norms to show us how to live in it.

This development can also be interpreted as the emergence of a new mechanism of social control used by the middle classes. As soon as people cease to be too concerned with promotion and become conscious of how little social control they have, they are able to keep the decision-making structures of technological society at a distance by giving a higher value to their private lives. The sexual revolution can then be seen as one of the mechanisms of a dual society in which one sphere of life is dominated by scientific and technological rationality and kept apart from the second sphere, which is open to conviviality and affectivity (which may be either real or illusory).

6. TOWARDS A NEW SEXUAL MORALITY OR A NEW ETHIC OF SOCIETY?

If my analyses are relevant, it should be possible to define the phenomenon of the sexual revolution. It is clearly related to a crisis in bourgeois ethics, which were governed by the aim of controlling the passions so that they would be subservient to the individual's achievement of his objectives. Confronted with affectivity and sexuality, economic and technological reason felt threatened by anxiety and this led society to develop a sexual morality in which Eros is subject to Logos while at the same time giving a high value to individual persons. The repressive aspect of this morality could not, however, continue to make itself felt in those parts of the world and among those social classes which were, in industrial society, based on a prosperous economy. The conviction that something new was being built could no longer justify this repression of sexuality and give it a high value. The resulting tension was greatest among the members of the social classes with little social power who had hardly any interest in advancing socially or economically, but who were really powerful in their private lives. These were the members of the upper middle classes.

Seen as symptoms, the sexual revolution points to the decline of bourgeois morality, which was a masculine morality based on self-control and subjecting affectivity to the building of a world. This revolution, however, asserts the value of the individual which is peculiar to the bourgeois morality and makes it clear that it is impossible to revert to an ethic of the sacralised body of the kind that we have inherited from the middle ages. The question that it asks of our society, in which family life, affectivity and economic and technological production are so distinct from each other is this: How can affective and sexual life be linked together with the technological, economic and political aspects of society? In other words, if the sexual revolution is not exclusively concerned with interpersonal relationships, but is a symptom related to a change in society, we are bound to ask how we are to live in a society in which our production, our power structures and even the way in which we think of our affectivity and our bodies are determined by technological structures. Of one thing we can be sure—what is involved in the sexual revolution is not only a 'sexual morality', but also an ethic of society. It is clear from an analysis of the sexual revolution that the sexual element cannot be separated from the socio-political element.

Translated by David Smith

Notes

1. This idea is outlined in a more general way in my book *Choix éthiques et conditionnement social* (Paris 1979), ET: *Liberation Ethics* (Philadelphia 1982). There are many presuppositions that can hardly be analysed in this article, as there are in any analysis of such ideological phenomena as the sexual revolution. When we examine the bourgeois morality, should we, for example, do what M. Foucault did in his *La Volonté de Savoir* (Paris 1976) and emphasise the technique of bourgeois power that is embodied in arguments about sexuality? Or should we follow J. van Ussel, *Sexualunterdrückung* (Hamburg 1970), and stress the repressive aspect? Authors frequently provide very different analyses. It is, for example, difficult to determine when 'history' is repeating itself or when a new phenomenon is occurring. How does bourgeois rationality differ from that of Saint Augustine? How is bourgeois control of the passions different from that of the Stoics? Or that of the bourgeois merchants from that of the Phoenicians? How does the pursuit of happiness in the eighteenth century differ from that practised by the Epicureans? When did the nuclear family really originate? When is a social custom no more than a reflection of what occurred in a previous period and when does it introduce a new element? For all these questions, see also P. Ariès *L'Enfant et les relations familiales sous l'ancien régime* (Paris 1960); J. L. Flandrin *Familles* (Paris 1976); J. Leclercq *Monks and Marriage: A Twelfth Century View* (New York 1982); E. Shorter *The Making of the Modern Family* (New York 1975; London 1976/1979); L. Stone *The Family, Sex and Marriage, England 1500–1800* (New York 1977); E. Zaretski *Capitalism, the Family and Personal Life* (New York 1975); J. Donzelot *La Police des familles* (Paris 1977). I have to thank my colleagues, Professor P. Delooz and Professor P. P. Druet for their suggestions and criticisms. M. Douglas *Natural Symbols, Explorations in Cosmology* (London 1970 and New York 1982), has shown how the way in which bodies and other 'natural symbols' are presented reflect social structures.

2. See I. Illich *Gender* (New York 1982) and J. L. Flandrin *Un Temps pour embrasser* (Paris 1983).

3. See J. Goudemet *Les Communautés familiales* (Paris 1963) and A. Jaccard *L'Exil intérieur* (Paris 1975).

4. See R. Pernoud *La Femme au temps des cathédrales* (Paris 1980).

5. See M. Foucault *La Volonté de savoir*, cited in note 1.

6. See S. Freud *The Future of an Illusion; Civilisation and its Discontents and other Works* (S.E. 21, 1961); Marcuse *Eros and Civilisation* (1955); A. Jaccard, the work cited in note 3.

7. The working classes experienced a 'sexual revolution' as early as the beginning of the nineteenth century when they became proletarian; see Shorter *The Making of the Modern Family*, cited in note 1, and Flandrin *Familles*, also cited in the same note.

8. Even now women do not analyse morality as men do; see C. Gilligan *In a Different Voice* (Boston 1982).

John Gagnon

Notes Toward an Understanding of the Transformation of Sexual Conduct

1. INTRODUCTION

THERE IS probably general agreement among most persons in Western societies that sexuality is different nowadays from what it was in the past. The fact of this agreement however does not usually consider whether all or only some aspects of sexuality have changed, how much difference there is between then and now, or indeed what the actual date might be in the past which serves as our baseline moment. Without a minimum specification of these issues it is impossible to thoughtfully try to understand the social and psychological processes through which various aspects of sexuality might have changed (if indeed they have).

It is important to note here that scientific representations of sexual conduct have a very short history, perhaps less than a century, and that the amount and cultural extent of these representations are limited. Data on sexual life is largely limited to Western, industrial societies and indeed the most extensive information concerns middle class populations in the United States. It might be argued as part of a larger theory of social evolution or cultural convergence that the direction of general social change among most societies is towards the models similar to the US and Western Europe, an evolution or convergence that would include models of sexuality. However, such hypotheses may not be confirmed. The rise of powerful cultural resistances to Western social patterns is evident in some parts of the non-Western world, resistances that may well preclude parallels to the sexual transformations observed in the West. Even in those cases where elements of western societies are admitted they may well become unrecognisable in new cultural contexts. Even within the European cultural area substantial differences in sexual conduct may occur among various nation States, even those with relatively similar patterns of urbanisation, industrialisation, technological development and governmental structure.

A further caveat must be added on the cultural-historical nature of the scientific enterprise with reference to sexuality even in Western societies. It is only since Freud and his contemporaries that we have accumulated a body of representations of sexuality, clinical case histories, surveys, life histories, laboratory studies, which meet the explanatory, technical and observational constraints of the scientific enterprise. At the same time it must be recognised that even those explanations, techniques, and observations that fall within this narrow envelope of time have been subjected to

11

considerable scrutiny and critique in search for ideological as well as scientific bias.

What needs to be understood is that during the same period (1890–1960) that there was a substantial transformation of the sexual world itself, the instruments of inquiry were themselves undergoing a parallel, but not isomorphic transformation. The forces that were re-shaping the character of sexual conduct also played a role in setting the conditions for the development of explanations of that conduct, delimiting the techniques of inquiry and making judgment on the accuracy of the resultant observations. However 'scientific' these representations of sexual life might have been or are now, they have also attained the status of alternative versions of the sexual life which are powerfully competitive with those based on traditional religious values, folk wisdom or utopian visions.

It is the changes in the processes of inquiry and changes in the objects of inquiry and the interactions between them that make an easy and direct interpretation of the 'data' on sexual life impossible. It is not only that the history of sex research is a history of changing techniques (Freud's clinical case studies, Havelock Ellis's life histories, Kinsey's surveys, Masters' and Johnson's laboratory observations) or changing representations of the facts (interpretative essays, quotations in print of a subject's statements, tables of percentages and statistics), but that researchers themselves were in the process of borrowing and inventing historically appropriate explanations for what they observed. To discuss the transformations of sexual conduct over the last century requires an understanding of the transformation of that special form of modern sexual conduct, sex research.

Having noted these issues, I would like to set them aside, to bracket them as it were, and examine some of the recent transformations in sexual conduct in the United States as they are represented in a variety of research traditions. Such an exercise is surely bounded by the cultural and historical constraints noted above, but work at this level retains its value as long as the provisional character of its arguments and the limited extent of its applicability are emphasized.

2. SEXUALITY: AREAS OF CHANGE AND STABILITY

There does exist, with reference to *some* aspects of sexuality in the United States, information from a variety of sources that provide some rough sense of what some of the directions of change have been since the 1930s and 1940s when minimally adequate sexual bookkeeping for this society began.

Pre-Marital Heterosexuality

There is a substantial body of evidence that, since the data reported in the Kinsey studies on white and largely youthful and college educated people (Kinsey *et al*, 1948, 1953), the incidence of pre-marital intercourse among young women has increased, that intercourse now occurs with more partners and starts at an earlier age for some segments of the population (for a summary of these changes see Chilman, 1979). For college going populations we can roughly date the beginning of the behavioral aspects of these changes to the early to middle 1960s. The first target cohort to examine would thus seem to be those born around 1945 and after, those at the front edge of the baby boom. Further increases in these measures of pre-marital sexuality have occurred since the mid-sixties and various recent important contextual social effects (e.g., the influence of larger numbers of sexually experienced peers, the availability of birth control) need also to be studied. Correlates of these changes have been increased rates of pre-marital pregnancy, pre-marital cohabitation, and the like (Chilman, 1980, Gagnon and Greenblat, 1978).

It is proper to note that these well documented changes in pre-marital heterosexuality of young women have been matters of considerable ideological conflict. The sexual property value of women and the control of reproductivity remain of considerable social concern and rises in these rates have usually been read as indicators of individual and collective moral collapse. This struggle for control over the sexuality of young women has largely obscured changes in the pre-marital heterosexuality of young men. Thus the fact that young men, at least since the 1940s are *less* likely to have their first coital experience with prostitutes and that the frequency of such intercourse has declined, and that there is some evidence that young men are acquiring patterns of pre-marital intercourse (both behaviorally and psychologically) similar to those of young women has excited little concern (Miller and Simon, 1974). None of these patterns of change are as yet well understood, though some links in the process are somewhat clarified. For instance, the relation between the decision to begin coitus and the availability of birth control appears to be near to zero, however the continuation of and the frequency of coitus are associated with the availability of contraception.

3. HOMOSEXUALITY

In another domain of sexuality there is evidence from many sources—the mass media, a few scientific studies, the existence of activist social movements, and the character of daily life (at least in some cities)—that gay men and lesbians have a different relation to the dominant heterosexual style in the United States than 20 years ago. One can locate changes over time among gay men and lesbians in the experience of self-identification, in forms of community participation, in the nature of emotional and intellectual and political commitments (for a review of the recent literature, see Gagnon, 1981). Most critically the definition of homosexuality and heterosexuality as polar opposites—the fact that our everyday conception of the one is predicated on the absence of the other—is in a preliminary state of collapse. The erosion of a hard boundary between homosexuality and heterosexuality means that the differences and similarities between both forms of conduct need to be readdressed with references to our concepts of the etiology of, motivations for and psychological adjustments related to sexual preference.

4. PUBLIC REPRESENTATIONS OF SEXUALITY

Certain aspects of sexuality have become more present in the landscape of everyday life. The availability of visual sexual stimuli, both public and private, chosen and unchosen, increased steadily between the mid-1950s and the late 1960s and exploded during the 1970s in the United States. There are probably few urban places without at least an X-rated book store or an X-rated movie theater. Television, subscription or free, programs or advertising, now brings into the home that which was not even on respectable newstands after World War II. The ubiquity of the change, the current sense of its routineness even by those who oppose it, makes the past not only dim and far away, but in some palpable way, false. The world in which the female and male nude were invisible, where nudist magazines were sold in brown wrappers from under the counter in special bookstores, in which the discreet underwear advertisements in a home sales catalogue were the acme of sensuality has largely disappeared. This was a world in which a major scientist could decide that women did not have an interest in visual sexual stimuli because there was something biologically different about their brains (Kinsey, 1953).

There is a fascination with evidence presented in support of these sexual changes—the moral and political debate is dominated by discussions of the topics of virginity, perversion and pornography. The mass media abets our narrow focus because it both foments our interest in change (novelty *is* news) and satisfies it in the same moment. Yet there are a number of equally important domains of sexual life in which the evidence for continuity is very substantial.

5. MARITAL INTERCOURSE

An examination of all of the reliable and even marginally reliable studies of marital intercourse in the US (which is the most common form of sexual activity in most societies) suggest that rates no matter how measured have remained remarkably stable over the last four decades (Gagnon, Greenblat and Roberts, 1979, Greenblat, 1982). Both the average number of times per month for the aggregate and the rate for various age groups in the population are exceptionally stable. There has been some drift upwards that can be attributed to improved contraception and reduced time in childbearing, but no substantial shifts beyond that. Despite the moral legitimacy of marital sex, the accessibility of partners, the proliferation of pro-sex marriage manuals, the availability of sex therapy, and the opportunity for derivative sexual arousal from the more titillating TV shows rates of marital coitus have changed very little. There is absolutely no evidence that this is because the rates have reached some biological maximum in the population.

6. MASTURBATION

What little data we have on masturbation suggests that the incidences and frequencies observed by Kinsey remain much the same today (Kinsey et al, 1953. Quartararo, Gagnon and Simon, 1982). Not only does this continuity stretch back to the 1950s, but to the 1920s among middle class populations. The differences that Kinsey observed between women and men also still seem to obtain until the very near present. No study suggests major increases in female masturbation either in terms of incidence or in terms of frequency.

As we are forced to take account of stability it becomes more difficult for us to evade the fact that we do not have good explanations of why change has or has not taken place. Further it raises issues about what the connections are between those aspects of sexual conduct that we have always assumed to have something to do with each other. If there is a substantial increase in the incidence and perhaps even the frequency of pre-marital sex why has marital sex even among younger populations remained much the same? If the world is more erotic in its everyday character why has the masturbation rate not changed?

A number of extremely serious theoretical and practical questions emerge from these apparent contradictions. Is it possible that the domain of sexual acts is not a singular and well connected set of activities which mutually influence each other and which have a common set of causes? Is it possible that just because acts all seem to involve the genitals that they are not all the same in their social or psychological meanings or origins? My colleague William Simon and I have already raised some questions about the degree to which events that are identified as sexual early in the life span are consequential for what is labelled and even experienced as sexual later in life. Thus there is doubt whether genital touching among infants is related to adult masturbation—the activity is not experienced similarly nor is its presence or absence causative of adult conduct (Simon and Gagnon, 1968).

An expanded version of that argument would suggest that various domains of adult sexual conduct may have little to do with each other (e.g. rates of or experience with masturbation may not directly influence patterns of pre-marital coitus), even though adults experience the conduct as part of the same general area of living. Our problem is that we do not have a very good theory of the origins and maintenance of what we call sexual conduct and this in itself constrains our ability to talk about sexual change or non-change. Our second is that we tend to look inward into the arenas of the sexual or the parasexual in order to find causal connections rather than to expand our vision to include a wide range of institutions and processes that are formative of and supportive of the sexual domains that exist today.

7. THE CHANGING CONTEXT OF SEXUAL LEARNING

A necessarily incomplete, but perhaps provocative way in which to suggest the character of this analytic enterprise, is to examine the roles of two quite disparate social institutions in transmitting and sustaining sexual learning. The first of these is the contemporary parent in the United States, the second, the social science theory and findings about sexuality which has been re-processed into the mass media about sexuality that is a ubiquitous part of sex education from grade school to University, the advice columns of mass media magazines and the press and books of facts, figures and stories about the 'way people live' sexually.

For some purposes these two institutions may be treated contrastively. The *authoritas* of the social science material is self-consciously modern, scientific, rational, disinterested seemingly quite at odds with the traditional, emotional, particularistic *authoritas* of the family. It should be noted, however, that the contemporary family should not be equated with the ideal typical family of the *gemeinschaft*, nor is modern social sexual science an exemplar of some abstract scientific enterprise. In practice both of these institutions in the United States are elements of an advanced industrial society—however their rights and privileges, their social *power* resides in their symbolic connection to these ideals of tradition versus modernity. In the debates over the proper role of the family and the educationist in the sexual education of children it is these claims of the ideal, rather than the world of practices which takes priority. However the practices themselves have a significant consequence for sexual conduct.

8. PARENTS' AND CHILDREN'S SEXUAL LEARNING

A reasonable body of recent research has focused on the role of the family in the United States in informing young children about sexuality. The findings of the most recent surveys about the amount and character of information transmitted by parents to these children would be uniformly depressing to those who want parents to be primary sex educators (Gagnon and Roberts, 1980). While parents universally report that they want to be helpful to their children, they felt unprepared and uneasy. They reported not knowing what to say as well as not knowing how to say it. This anxiety extended not only to issues of the morality of sexual conduct as well as to matters of reproductive and erotic knowledge. Perhaps most apparent was their fear that sex information had the potential to provoke sexual conduct. That is, they felt that the information that they gave to their children, particularly as the latter approached puberty, was likely to be converted into overt conduct.

The most telling findings were those answers to the questions about the relation between intercourse and pregnancy. When parents were asked when children should be told about the fact that the fetus grows inside the mother they commonly gave an early age even though there was evidence that many of them had not yet given this information to their children who were over that age. When asked when children should be told about intercourse and its connection with pregnancy this was always at some much later age. Those with five year olds said at ten, those with ten year olds, 13 or 14. These findings are correlative with those that indicate that parents have not spoken to their ten and eleven year olds about such soon-to-be-upon-them events as masturbation and menstruation. Further, parents report traditional gender specific responses to the sex education needs and the potential sexual lives of boys and girls. Girls need to know about menstruation, boys do not; knowledge about and the practice of masturbation when it is approved is more appropriate for boys than girls.

It is evident from this study and others that these practices are not much different when we contrast parents by education, class, race, religion or marital status. A gross but not inaccurate summary of recent research is that mothers tend to provide information to children, both male and female more than fathers. Such information provision tends to be infrequent, is more about reproduction than eroticism, declines with the age of the child, and is more often initiated by the child rather than by the parent.

The important issue here is the similarity of these findings to what we would have found thirty years ago in terms of parental participation in the sexual education of their children. These are findings from studies conducted in the late 1970s which included a number of youthful parents, that is parents who were born after 1955 and who were reared in the 1960s. The lack of differences between this study and the past and in the study between the younger and older parents does not suggest basic changes in these patterns of parental conduct about sexuality. This is not to say that other important changes may not have occurred in the other domains which we viewed as important to sexuality—changes in gender role training and expectations, changes in the way parents teach children about their bodies, changes in the ways in which the emotions are expressed and constrained, changes in the ways in which parents approach the questions of moral responsibility. However a review of whatever literature that exists suggests that these domains of parenting have not changed a great deal either. Perhaps the one domain that has changed is the larger number of children who have been reared in non-nuclear households for at least part of the youthful period. Thus the experience of parental divorce, single parenting, the processes of parental dating and remarriage and step-parenting are more common and therefore might influence the range of life style options thought appropriate. At the same time it is possible that some may acquire a preference for more traditional styles from living unconventional childhoods.

Contemporary parents in the United States may indeed influence the sexual lives of their children, but the evidence for the degree and in what ways remains obscure. What we do know is that the processes are commonly indirect and rarely through the provision of reproductive and erotic knowledge. The absence of teaching may be consequential, but primarily by creating an informational vacancy into which other agents can take up residence. In addition it is clear that the family institution is probably not the major active force behind changes in the sexual lives of young people. Further to the degree that the family remains a de-sexualised institution between parents and children it may remain so in the relation between husband and wife. The fears of the sexual that seem to pervade parent-child relations (take no risk of change by obeying rules of silence) may also characterise familial sexual relations in general. Whatever evidence there is suggests that husbands and wives do not communicate about sexuality and that their sexual lives are also governed more by silence than speech (Greenblat, 1982). An understanding of the reasons why men and women do not communicate about sexuality, a failure of communication that may be leading to low rates of marital sexuality may also lead us to some fruitful ideas about why they do not communicate about sexuality with their children.

This absence of input about eroticism by parents may well be one reason that peers tend to dominate the social context in which young people learn about erotic sexuality. However parents are not only important in what they fail to do but in the fact that they reinforce traditional gender role values. By training their male and female children differently they set up the conditions for a division between young men and women in adolescence, a division that allows separate peer worlds to emerge. In these two separate and unequal worlds boys learn about genital sexuality and masturbation while girls learn about love and the importance of boys. Parental absence allows peers to control erotic learning and practice, parental presence reinforces traditional gender role stereotypes (Gagnon and Simon, 1973). As parents have grown less powerful in the lives of their adolescent children, peers have grown more important. What may be learned from this is that when parents' views are heavily reinforced, as in the case of gender roles, parents retain their significance, when they are both absent and resisted, as in the case of erotic learning, other forces take control.

9. THE SOCIAL SCIENCE MEDIA

Beginning in the 1920s but accelerating over the last decades social science research in all areas has served as the basis for and the grist for the social science journalist or the journalist social scientist. During this same period the margin between scientific social science and popular social science has become eroded. Thus surveys are now conducted by magazines, some of them meeting many of the technical rules of survey research, and first publications of these materials are scheduled as part of the magazines' fare. In most cases the studies are close to worthless and in other cases harmful because they falsify the world, however the need of the media machinery for new social facts to place between the advertisements is nearly endless (Gagnon and Greenblat, 1978).

New sexual facts are prime candidates for inclusion in such media reports and commentary. What is important about them is that they often offer alternative forms of sexual conduct both in terms of what persons do and why they might do them. Thus the mass of sexual information and theory that has come from the social sciences has been to increasingly conventionalise what were previously forms of sexual deviance. One need only examine the sexuality textbooks meant for college students or the books for parents and children to recognise the themes that emphasise the tolerance of difference as well as the inclusion of that which was once considered different as being inside the orbit of the usual.

A number of strategies have been adopted to reduce previously important moral or mental health differences. The first has been to point out that what was formerly valued and formerly disvalued have much in common—the Shylock strategy. Do not gay men and lesbians also hold jobs, care for their parents, love their children, pay their taxes, share leisure pursuits in the same manner as the dominant heterosexual class? The second has been the claims of common origin or purpose, is not prostitution simply just another way of making money, is it not merely just another occupation such as those of doctors, lawyers, nurses? Even motivational histories can look the same—the young woman has pre-marital sex for love, belonging, fulfilment just as the young woman joins the Girl Scouts. What were clear cut differences between the virtuous and the corrupt tend to dissolve. Masturbation and surrogates in sex therapy are now the necessary adjuncts of sexual health in many clinics around the country (LoPiccolo and Heiman, 1977).

These alternative visions of the sexual which take their force from the relativitic authority of modern science rarely have immediate effects on sexual conduct of individuals. They are insufficiently compelling for that consequence. What they may do is to make the population far more tolerant, they provide explanations for the conduct of the sexually 'deviant' and give evidence for their moral worth, and in some cases they influence the police functions of the society. They change the contexts for sexual conduct and how various forms of sexual conduct is evaluated and perhaps in the long run may have consequences for another generation's sexuality, but they have limited short run effects.

10. THE COMPLEXITY OF SEXUAL CHANGE

What is suggested by this short discussion of two contemporary sources of sexual learning is the complexity of the processes of the acquisition and maintenance of sexual conduct and the competition that exists among the agents of communication and the messages they send. Not only do we have to concern ourselves with communicators and messages, but we have to attend to issues of changing individuals over the life span. We cannot limit our interests to the narrowly sexual since there is unimpeachable evidence that factors both close to the sexual (e.g. beliefs about the body or gender role learning) and factors that are far more distant (e.g. consumption desires) have consequences for our sexual lives. Finally we must confront the fact that various components of sexual conduct are the result of quite different causal configurations. The gender differences historically found in masturbation may remain relatively unchanged during adolescence because it is linked to traditional peer group learning opportunities—pre-marital intercourse may take on a more similar pattern among young men and women because of the role of sex in the formation of intimate heterosocial relations before marriage. What may affect one aspect of sexuality may not affect another.

As important for understanding the moral dimensions of sexual conduct is an understanding of the socio-political forces which define one form of behavior as sickness and another as health. One of the major transformations of the last thirty years has been the steady change of labels for many forms of sexual conduct from sin to sickness to deviance to unconventionality to instances of mental health. Because these changes have taken place so rapidly, fervent supporters of each point of view can be found not only in the market place of ideas, but also in the churches, the legislatures and the police stations. The political processes by which various aspects of sexuality have had their moral and legal labels changed is part of the context of acquiring and maintaining sexual conduct.

Perhaps most problematic of all is the conception that the domain of the 'sexual' is itself an historical-cultural construction without the timeless or universal character that could make it amenable to robust moral judgment.

References

Atwood, Joan D., Gagnon, John H. and Simon, William *Masturbation in Adolescence and Young Adulthood*, mimeo. 1982, 40 pp.

Chilman, Catherine *Adolescent Sexuality in a Changing Society* (Washington, DHEW Publication (NIH) 1979) pp. 79–1426.

Chilman, Catherine, ed. *Adolescent Pregnancy and Childrearing* (Washington, DHEW Publication (NIH) 1980) pp. 81–2077.

Gagnon, John H. *Human Sexualities* (Glenview, Ill., Scott Foresman 1977).

Gagnon, John H. 'Books from the Gay Male and Lesbian Bookshelf' *American Journal of Orthopsychiatry* 51, 3, 1981, 560–568.

Gagnon, John H. and Greenblat, Cathy S. *Life Designs* (Glenview, Ill., Scott Foresman 1978).

Gagnon, John H., Greenblat, Cathy S. and Roberts, Elizabeth J. 'Stability and Change in Rates of Marital Intercourse' a paper presented at the *Annual Meetings of the International Academy of Sex Research* Toronto 1978.

Gagnon, John H. and Roberts, Elizabeth J. 'Parents' Messages to Pre-Adolescent Children About Sexuality' in Samson, J. M., ed. *Childhood and Sexuality* (Montreal, Editions Etudes Vivantes 1981) pp. 276–286.

Gagnon, John H. and Simon, William *Sexual Conduct* (Chicago, Aldine 1973).

Greenblat, Cathy S. 'Accounting for Marital Intercourse' a paper presented at the *Annual Meetings of the American Sociological Association*, San Francisco 1982.

Kinsey, A. C., *et al. Sexual Behavior in the Human Male* (Philadelphia, Saunders 1948).

Kinsey, A. C. *et al. Sexual Behavior in the Human Female* (Philadelphia, Saunders 1953).

LoPiccolo, Joseph and Heiman, Julia 'Cultural Values and the Therapeutic Definition of Sexual Function and Dysfunction' *Journal of Social Issues* 33, 2, 1977, 166–183.

Miller, Patricia Y. and Simon, William 'Adolescent Sexual Behavior: Context and Change' *Social Problems* 22, 1, 1974, 58–76.

Simon, William and Gagnon, John H. 'On Psychosexual Development' in Goslin, D. G., ed. *The Handbook of Socialization Theory and Research* (Chicago, Rand McNally 1968) pp. 733–752.

Trussell, James and Westoff, Charles F. 'Contraceptive Practice and Trends in Coital Frequency' *Family Planning Perspectives* 12, 3, 1981, 246–249.

Sabino Acquaviva

Sexual Behaviour and Social Change in a Society in Transition: The Case of Italy

1. INTRODUCTION: WHAT IS SPECIAL ABOUT ITALY

THE SEXUAL behaviour of Italian society has changed substantially over the period of the past twenty years. This is of course also true of other European countries, but the case of Italy does present special features.

In the first place, the change here concerns a country which has relatively recently emerged from being under-developed. This means that previous sexual behaviour (at least in parts of the country) was typical of a backward society. We shall see later what this means.

In the second place, the change has come about in an unusually brief span of time, since the economic and social growth which have brought the country from under-development to development have been equally rapid. The consequences of this rapidity of change in the field of sexual behaviour have been many and specific.

In the third place, the change has come about in a society which is not homogenous in either its economic, social or cultural features. This means that the results of development (including its consequences for sexual behaviour) have varied greatly from region to region and only later developed similarities on a national level. The normal difference between town and country, typical of all developed and industrialised countries, is exacerbated in Italy by the consistent difference between North and South, which is much greater than that found in other European countries such as France or Great Britain, which have been united and independent for much longer than Italy.

2. THE MODEL OF UNDERDEVELOPMENT FROM WHICH THE CHANGE IN SEXUAL BEHAVIOUR STEMS

To understand the evolution of sexual behaviour, we need first to sum up briefly the cultural characteristics of this model of underdevelopment.

Like all societies, that of Italy was organised according to a system of values accepted by the majority of its members (socialised through agencies such as the schools and the family), and to an institutional system characteristic of an underdeveloped, subsistence, economic structure. The system of legitimisation (values), the system of socialisation (integration into the system), the institutional and power structure (and hence social organisation), and the economic system that was the function of the first three (and vice versa), were all so to speak locked one into the other.[1] But at this time the structure was also rigidly family-orientated: political power, law, religion, education, all revolved round the family: so the whole system was centred on the primacy of the family and of the man as head of the family.

This was more true of the South than of the North, more of the towns than of the country, and, of course more of agricultural regions than of the (very few) industrialised zones. The family system was linked to a mixed structure made up of magic and religion, Christian-pagan in the Mediterranean mode, over which—especially in the South—Christianity had been spread like a layer of varnish.

In this situation, social sins had long been those committed against paternal authority, against the husband, the master. Socialisation, furthermore, reinforced a system based on male authority, in which women, who played a subordinate role, brought their children up to obey. All this went with an individualism which regarded society as the enemy of the family and of the individual.[2]

'The individual, shut into his family, often felt alone in the face of the arbitrary forces of the society that surrounded him.'[3] All this led to the image of the man as protector-in-chief; hence machismo, male chauvinism, the image of woman as holy mother, the whole picture of a particular family structure.[4] Finally, until the break-up of the economic structures of depression, Italian society was a society on the defensive, shut in and static in matters of:

(a) the family and sexual behaviour;
(b) the culture and values on which sex and the family were based;
(c) the entrepreneurial spirit and economic development.

Sexual behaviour was 'blocked'; sexual and moral deviation in adultery or similar matters were socially condemned, but with the dual standard which meant that in sexual matters, the man 'could'. Hence sexual repression and male chauvinism went hand in hand.

3. THE DEVELOPMENT MODEL AND CHANGING SOCIAL CUSTOMS: THE GENERAL FRAME OF REFERENCE

But the sexual model (and the overall social model) that goes with underdevelopment reaches breaking-point with a certain degree of economic, political and cultural pressure, and this is what happened in Italy—sooner in the North than in the South, but in the end over the whole country.

As a result of the two world wars, but more markedly in the period after the second, society became dualistic in all senses of the word. Traditional values rubbed shoulders with new ones, development with underdevelopment. Energy coexisted with indolence, the entrepreneurial spirit with stagnation. Inefficiency and 'effectivism' became the twin spirits animating Italian society. This period saw the emergence of a liberal-catholic culture, an Italian and Catholic version of the Protestant work ethic inspired by Weber, seeking to safeguard the family while proceeding with its own sort of 'liberalisation'.

But this phase was overtaken by a too rapid development, one, as has already been noted, specifically Italian in character. Some areas, once rigidly dominated by the family concept, with completely traditional sexual mores, underwent exceptional degrees of development: one such was Gargano. This was a region which had no roads at the end of the first World War; in 1951 its average per capita income was 100 dollars a year: by 1981 this has risen to 3,000 dollars, a thirty-fold increase in thirty years. The effects of this on values and customs can only be compared to those of an earthquake.[5] This phenomenon has of course been observed in all developing countries, if not to quite the same extent.

C

Added to this development was the fact that millions of Italians emigrated from the South to the North.

In such a situation, the traditional system, including that of moral values, loses its force and disintegrates, largely because local social micro-structures, in small towns and villages, tend to break up: this system in crisis is then assailed by the mass media and consumerism—a consumerism whose impact, because of the rapidity of change, falls directly on to a culturally underdeveloped society.

This also explains the crisis of traditional religiosity of the popular kind, but also that of religious practice in general. On the moral level, this produces a prevalence of permissive and consumerist attitudes, bringing an emphasis on sexual matters similar to that found in the rest of Europe: the clamour for free abortion, gay liberation movements, feminist movements and culture.

This then is the general, overall, frame of reference within which the changes in sexual behaviour have come about.[6] Let us now try to examine some of the details of the phenomenon a little more closely, starting with the passage from a general and sexual morality of underdevelopment to the present one characteristic of a consumer society. In this society the dominant social models, that of Catholicism and that of Marxism, are undergoing a process of constant erosion through the emergence of an empirical cultural model, problematical, possibilist: in short, scarcely ideological, that goes with industrial development and the spread of education.[7]

4. THE PRIMACY OF THE BODY AND NEW VALUES: THE MOTORS OF CHANGE IN SEXUAL BEHAVIOUR

The need to satisfy the most imperative material needs, which belongs to a subsistence economy and one of underdevelopment (in the moral sphere too), is turned into a cultivation of the body, an assertion of the primacy of the body and of new needs, previously unknown in Italian society.

In a sense, one could say that the *a priori* norms of the prescriptive society Italy is growing out of are tending to become weaker, or even to disappear, to be replaced by norms which express a different experience of one's own body as well as a partly different system of values. I would say that what is emerging is a philosophy based on the primacy of the body, on *a posteriori* norms (resulting from personal experience), that is, on needs which 'make' their own norms. As in general terms we are moving from a subsistence economy to a 'free-for-all' consumerism, and as certain aspects of Italian consumerism demonstrate its origins in an economy of poverty and subsistence, so the liberalisation of sexual behaviour shows traces of the previous minutely prescriptive society in moral matters. The family of course lives on, but it is 'weaker' than in the past. Society moves on a 'continuum' that goes from the traditional family to lives lived apart, cut off from others, solitary, either because people have opted to cut family ties by moving towards an 'open family', which does not necessarily require sexual fidelity, or because, as many have done, they have chosen to live alone. It is in this psychological-cultural climate of sexual liberalisation—starting from a situation of underdevelopment and social control greater than that generally found in already developed European countries—that the various libertarian movements are reaching out beyond the limits expected by those who have studied the question: gay liberation movement, women's liberation movements, other more broadly 'underground' movements, all are growing fast and furiously.

The importance of acting according to the dictates of one's conscience is generally accepted, in Catholic circles as well. On the popular level, this produces a transformation of everyone into 'being his own man'. In this framework, the whole culture surrounding sexual behaviour is completely changed: 'there is a new way of talking, of loving, of finding one's place in society, of making friends, of living together: a whole new attitude to life and to its meaning, as well to the meaning of death and political involvement. In short, the whole way of living and thinking has changed, as has the cultural frame of reference'.[8]

It is impossible in a few pages to give an account of the thousand details that go to make up the various major changes, and how they revolve round the change in sexual behaviour, a change towards new directions and meanings rooted in such a different past.

However, to illustrate the change through one of its aspects, one could say that an eros once sublimated in a popular religiosity that was very concrete, material, almost physical—as the Italian form was—with a strong element of sensuality, has become an unsublimated eros drawing all aspects of life to itself. These aspects, in which the physical is more than ever dominant, are concentrated—to a large extent, at least—on the libido, on eros: so the liberalisation of sex has no ulterior point of reference; sex has become an 'end in itself' with no further meaning. Yet there are many points of continuity between the underdeveloped past and the values and culture of a developed country. The former obsession with sex, for example, has become a sexual obsession for liberation, in which sex is a symbol, an objective: or perhaps, the obsession is a quest for a specific meaning to life, a material mode of living. We now have a society in which—more than before and in more different ways—what is true is equated with what *is*, but it is also a society in which all the members are undergoing substantial, bodily changes, in the sense that the psyche and the culture are continually being moulded, taken apart and put together again by the processes of a technology and an economic development for which they were not prepared: a similar process can be seen at work, even more violently and consistently, in those countries that are still underdeveloped.

In Italy, however, the old conditions the new and 'insinuates itself' into it, in a very specifically Mediterranean way. For example, the rejection of work, which has grown in recent years under the influence of a certain type of Marxist culture, is largely an inherited residue of the reluctance to work characteristic of certain aspects of the culture of underdevelopment. So, in order to understand the evolution of sexual behaviour, one must go back to the roots of this society. As I have already remarked, to regard the body as the space within which one lives and feels is an ancient Mediterranean trait, leading to the development of sexual polytheism in this space, which in itself is not exclusive to Italian society. What has happened is that this society has seen the emergence of a different importance given to the body in the overall system of values, which in turn has given a new position and a new meaning to libido and eros: sexual 'liberation' is seen as an appropriation of their own bodies and minds by women and men alike.

5. SOME VERIFICATIONS OF THE THEORIES ADVANCED: INQUIRIES

For example, one indication of these developments emerges from a recent 'indirect' inquiry into the behaviour of married women, with particular reference to adultery. Although the inquiry dealt with a highly industrialised part of Northern Italy and a socially cultured and relatively affluent section of society, its results do demonstrate a general tendency.[9]

The ladies questioned in this piece of research were asked to say: 'How many of your friends or acquaintances, in percentage terms, could be considered habitual adulteresses?'. Two hundred and sixty-one of those interviewed, equal to nearly 83%, gave a figure of between none and 40%; 34, equal to 10%, said between 40 and 80%; 15, that is 4%, claimed that 'all' or 'nearly all' the ladies they knew well could be counted among the 'habitual adulteresses'. A good many more gave higher percentage figures when the question asked referred to occasional adultery.

When the inquiry went deeper into the motives that led people to commit adultery, many of the psychological, practical and ideological factors that I have discussed emerged. Furthermore, it was generally felt that in the context of an 'open family', sexual infidelity did not imply infidelity in love or a denial of marriage. While the above refers to the more affluent and more developed sections of society, sexual behaviour in other sections is moving along the same lines, though at a different speed and in slightly different ways, with differences between the North and the South (where sexual freedom is less readily accepted), and between rich and poor (liberalisation being likewise less accepted among the latter).

For example, an inquiry in 1977 found that only 14% of women and 41% of men admitted to having or having had an adulterous relationship.[10] But the question was *direct* and so of little significance: in most cases the women did not seem to be telling the truth, for obvious reasons. Furthermore, the fact that even the deep South is changing emerges from some questions put there,[11] at an interval of nearly thirteen years, to the same constituency, about pre-marital sexual relations. To the question whether a man could respect a woman who had pre-marital relations, 10.47% said 'Yes' in 1965, whereas by 1978 the number had gone up to 26.75%. The numbers who said 'It depends on the circumstances' had also gone up, from 21.99% to 27.25%. This, I repeat, is in an area formerly among the poorest and most remote of the South: the contrast with Northern Italy is marked.

6. EVOLUTION OF THE EROS, DEATH, RELIGION POLARITY IN A CHANGING SOCIETY

There is, as I have said, an overall change in the system of values and codes of behaviour; sex is changing (liberalised), so is the image of death (denied) and religion (more personalised, less extrovert). I should like to stress the importance of the connection between sexual liberalisation and the evolution of the image of death, which is no longer tied to a precise and deeply held understanding of religion and the life after death: a most significant connection in a Mediterranean type of society in which, only a few years ago, the cult of the dead was particularly important.

There is less certainty about death because there is less religious conviction: this diminution of religiosity is closely linked to sexual liberalisation and to the vertical drop (consequent on liberalisation) in religious sublimation of love and eros, especially among adolescents. In short, the growth of unsublimated eros goes, through the crisis in values, with the expulsion of the idea of death: which is perhaps responsible for the cultural note of this society being one of anxiety. With sex liberalised and death placed at a remove, Italian society, perhaps like that of all developed countries, sees men and women looking for mechanisms of reassurance that are hard to find: an attempt to rediscover at least a psychologically transcendent dimension in everyday life. This dimension, as many researches have shown, is found, or at least an attempt is made to find it, in an eros often mixed with an underlying mockery of religion.

7. SOME CONSIDERATIONS IN CONCLUSION

At this point perhaps the discussion could have been brought to an end. So far, I have tried to produce evidence to show what the new motivations and characteristics of sexual behaviour are, but within the general confines of a predominantly cultural approach; other factors, such as the structural and technical conditions of change, urbanisation, the spread of education, economic development, consumerism, class mobility, the change from dogmatism to empirical specifics in the political debate, the development of a technico-scientific culture, youth protest and 'underground' movements, secularisation, etc., have been noted, but not dealt with in detail, as this would inevitably have produced an analysis that would have overlapped with others that have already been made about (and in) other countries.

However, I should like to sum up with regard to three factors: the *profile* of the changes, their *consequences*, and some possible pointers for the *future*.

(a) The profile

Italian society, then, is one in which religion is tending to be pushed into the background and the traditional values of eros are partly evolving and partly taking on more obvious cultural manifestations: a society is being formed in which the direct chain of reference between sex, libido, eros (understood in its wide sense, to include friendship) and social structure is becoming of primary importance. Within this framework (in which the body becomes an instrument of language and dialogue) other forms of cultural expression, such as art (beginning with the cinema), are moving in the same direction. But the use of the body in this new framework of reference often tends to be disorganised and to move in a psychological space dominated by insecurity and anxiety. To sum up, this is a society in which images of the world, of society, of politics, of love, derive consistently from eros and the body, and 'deny' death.

(b) The consequences

The structures linked to sexual behaviour are changing, beginning with the family, which in this respect has become open, more based on simple non-institutionalised living together: we are moving to a freedom of affective relationships and a permissive family which, even from early childhood, is an image of society. Then family structure is duplicated in social structures, in the unions, in school, in university, and so (in eros, in the family and in society) the individualist characteristics, as opposed to civic (both traditional and modern in this respect), with some traces of the old family-centred attitude, clearly emerge. The emphasis on the family and the 'amoral' individualism of underdeveloped society, anti-social in many of its tendencies (as well as restrictive in its rules), has been turned inside out like a glove in Italian industrial society, and so we have moved to a permissive individualism and family-centredness, libertarian but—often— equally hostile to society at large.

Italian society, then, as I have said, is going through the same experiences as other industrial societies, but under the influence of its own particular roots. But how far can its behaviour be called 'libertarian'? Is the whole of society 'libertarian' on the sexual level? Statistical data and field researches would seem to show that we are in a transitional phase, one in which we have moved (or are moving), at least in some sectors, into the (at least partial) overthrow of traditional structures, but without any clear alternative scheme of overall behaviour emerging.

(c) The future

This then, is a society with no clear plans for its future: there are no precise lines accepted by the majority, perhaps because there is no clear view of the role of the family, or of the meaning of eros and sex. As time goes on, sex as a consumer product, or eros as the guiding principle of life, become ever more important principles of society. It is a society in which the fact that it has moved from a state of underdevelopment to one of development with great rapidity has meant that values such as efficiency or response to social needs are not fully taken to heart, or have not been yet; such values belong to other advanced societies which have reached a similar stage of development, but which have taken two hundred years to do so instead of thirty, such as Germany or Great Britain. Which, as we have seen, in matters of eros, sex and 'ultimate values', makes a great difference.

Translated by Paul Burns

Notes

1. Various *La modernizzazione sperata* (Naples 1979) p. 8.
2. *Ibid.* p. 11.
3. *Ibid.*
4. S. Acquaviva, G. Eisermann *La montagna del sole. Il Gargano: quattordici anni di storia fra due inchieste (1965–79)* (Rome² 1982) pp. 158ff.
5. *Ibid.* p. 156.
6. There are no recent works on the sexual behaviour of the Italians, apart from the already old G. Caletti *et. al. Il comportamento sessuale degli italiani* (Bologna 1976). See, however, G. Fabris, R. Davis *Rapporto sul comportamento sessuale degli italiani* (Milan 1978). There are notes on customs in N. Aspesi *Amore e famiglia*, in Various *Il trionfo del privato* (Bari 1980); on the dismembering of traditional models in *Il seme religioso della rivolta* ed. C. Lanzetti, L. Mauri (Milan 1979); Various *Ritratto di famiglia anni ottanta* (Bari 1981); G. Milanesi *et. al. Oggi credono cosi* (Turin 1981); on the South, see, *inter alia*, Lanzetti and Mauri, the work cited above; and especially, Various *La modernizzazione sperata*, cited in note 1, for the Abruzzi, and Acquaviva and Eisermann, the work cited in note 4, for the Puglia. On married women, see the data given in M. Rusconi 'L'adulterio femminile' in *L'espresso* 34 (1983), which gives the results of a still unpublished inquiry.
7. S. Acquaviva *In principio era il corpo* (Rome 1983), in particular the Introduction.
8. The work cited in note 1, p. 27.
9. Rusconi, the article cited in note 6, p. 35.
10. Fabris and Davis, the work cited in note 6, p. 121.
11. In Lanzetti and Mauri, the work cited in note 6; see in particular G. Milanesi 'Concezioni e comportamenti sessuali' pp. 153–211.

Rudolf Siebert

The Frankfurt School:
Enlightenment and Sexuality

THE CRITICAL theory of subject, society and history carries on the spirit of modern Enlightenment.[1] The critical theory as it developed from H. Horkheimer, Th. W. Adorno and W. Benjamin over L. Löwenthal, H. Marcuse, E. Fromm and A. Sohn-Rethel to J. Habermas, includes in itself the heritage of bourgeois, Marxian and Freudian enlightenment and emancipation.[2] The critical theorists understand enlightenment as the attempt to free people from their fears and to make them into masters of their fate. Critical theorists see the sexual enlightenment, emancipation and revolution as an integral part of the European Enlightenment movement. In this essay we concentrate on the critical theory in so far as it explores the sexual enlightenment and emancipation.

1. DIALECTIC

While the critical theorists have an affirmative attitude toward modern enlightenment, they are, nevertheless, also keenly aware of its inner dialectic.[3] Enlightenment can turn against itself and increase fears and dependence. Bourgeois enlightenment turned into guillotine, positivism and fascism; Marxian enlightenment into Stalinism; and Freudian enlightenment into Pavlovianism and Skinnerianism. But instead of being discouraged by this dialectic of enlightenment, critical theorists reflect it into their theory and precisely thereby are able to overcome it and to strengthen whatever is true and good in the modern emancipation process. Also the sexual enlightenment and emancipation has its inner dialectic, which is creatively to be overcome. In this study we follow the critical theory as it criticises the dialectic of sexual emancipation and tries to find remedies for it.

2. REASON

In Modernity, as in Antiquity before, enlightenment means subjectification: Reduction of all social arrangements to subjective reason.[4] Thus from Horkheimer, the founder of the critical theory, to Habermas, who continues it in the sign of the new paradigm of communicative praxis, critical philosophers have opposed Neo-Thomism and any other conservative ontological attempt to restore more or less naively objective reason, which

27

fell victim to modern enlightenment.[5] To critical theorists a new moral-theological concept like 'ontic sin' in sexual matters appears as relic of traditional thought characterised by the premodern mythical confusion between nature and culture, if not as mere cover for the seldom complete suppression of the sexual instinct in Western Civilisation and the chronic dishonesty connected with this.

But the dialectical philosophers do therefore not yield to subjective reason, more precisely instrumental reason.[6] Science cannot tell us why it is better to love than to hate, except that it may be better for business. It cannot give us a final interpretation or orientation in sexual matters or in any other issue of moral concern. Horkheimer and Adorno criticise most rigorously subjective reason out of the ironically alienated perspective of an objective reason, which disintegrated with the decentralisation of the religious-metaphysical world views in the process of modernisation, rationalisation, enlightenment, and disenchantment.[7] If objective reason can be rediscovered at all, then this can happen only through precisely such ironical-dialectical critique of subjective reason: *via negativa*.

For the time being, Horkheimer and Adorno can do no more than to emphasise subjective as practical, moral reason against instrumental reason in sexual as in all other matters of human concern. Habermas stresses subjective as communicative reason against functional reason. Practical and communicative reason are the subjective foundation of religion and morality. At present nothing threatens religious systems of interpretation and orientation more than the pathological subordination of practical under instrumental rationality, for which critical theorists try to find a remedy. Therefore, Horkheimer, Adorno, Benjamin and Marcuse are very much opposed to any alliance between religion and positivism in sexual or any other matter of moral concern.[8]

3. THEOLOGY

As the critical sociologists move between theology and philosophy on one hand and science on the other hand, they are open in principle for the possible truths contained in religious world views, particularly Judaism and Christianity: Creation as self-negation, original sin, second commandment, messiah, redemption, communicative ethics.[9] They try to rescue such truths by introducing them into the realm of the secular. This explains why critical theorists do sometimes take sides with theological ethics and ecclesiastical teaching against the sexual revolution, e.g. Horkheimer's support of Paul VI's encyclical 'Humanae Vitae'.[10]

Critical theory as such contains a theological dimension.[11] Horkheimer understands theology as hope for absolute justice. For Horkheimer as well as for Adorno and Benjamin no genuine morality is possible without theology. In the midst of the eclipse of reason, the critical theorists hold on to the emphatic notion of absolute truth, which is not possible without the prophetic and messianic God who guarantees it.[12] What is communicated to youth concerning moral impulses without reference to a Transcendent becomes a matter of mere subjective taste and mood, as well as its opposite.[13] For the critical theorists also sexuality is a matter of justice, truth, moral impulses and Transcendence.

4. SELF-UNDERSTANDING

The dialectical sociologists have traced the sexual enlightenment throughout modernity, but particularly through the nineteenth and twentieth centuries.[14] The sexual emancipation did not start in the 1960s and it has not ended with the 1970s. The sexual revolution has become a rather permanent one, certainly since the work of S. Freud, World War I and the 'wild' 1920s, which transformed deeply the sexual mores of liberal capitalistic society. On the shoulders of I. Kant, G. W. F. Hegel, K. Marx and Freud, the critical theorists have not only observed, described and analysed the sexual enlightenment, but also actively directed and corrected it. In a certain sense in the critical theory the sexual emancipation has come to its self-understanding and self-critique.

5. SEXUAL RELATIONSHIP

From its very beginning dialectical philosophy identified the sexual as species relationship.[15] As such the sexual relationship is situated on the organic, anthropological and sociological level. Critical philosophy contains a dialectical biology, anthropology and sociology of sexuality.

Dialectical biology determines the sexual relationship as reproduction of the species.[16] The species relationship is nothing else than the procreation of the individual through the death of another individual. After the one individual has produced itself as another individual, it dies off. Sexuality is the most differentiated and highest function of the organism. Sexuality and death are closely interconnected.

The species relationship is process. It begins with the sexual need of the individual. The need arises from the fact that the individual is, as singular being, not adequate to its genus and that it is at the same time the identical relationship of the genus to itself and that it is both of these in unity. Thus the individual has the feeling of insufficiency. Therefore the genus in the individual is the dialectical tension against the inadequacy of its singular reality. The genus in the individual is the drive to achieve in the partner of the other sex its self-feeling; to integrate itself through the union with the other; and through this mediation to close together the genus with itself and thus to bring it into immediate existence. That happens in the genus act or in copulation.

In dialectical anthropological perspective the species relationship of humans rests on the biological differentiation of the sexes.[17] On the one hand the sexual relationship is the individual's subjectivity, which remains one with itself in the feeling of social morality, erotic love, faithfulness, honor, etc. The sexual relationship does not proceed to the extreme of purposive universality: To society, state, history, art, religion, philosophy and science. It is limited to marriage and family. On the other hand, the sexual relationship is the activity, which in the individual moves into the opposition of universal, objective interests and his or her own particular existence and external world. The species activity realises those universal interests in this particular existence and produces them as unity. The sexual relationship achieves in marriage and family its spiritual and socio-ethical significance and determination.

According to dialectical sociology the species relationship is, as marriage, the immediate socio-ethical unit.[18] First of all, marriage contains the element of natural vivacity in its totality, namely the reality of the human genus and its process. But beyond this, in the self-consciousness of the marriage partners and their communicative praxis, the unity of the sexes, which is merely in itself and therefore existentially only external, is transformed into self-conscious sexual, erotic and ethical love. The first element in this love is that the lover does not want to be an independent person for himself or herself. In so far as the lover is such an independent person, he or she feels deficient and incomplete. The second moment in love is that the lover gains himself or herself in another person and is thereby enriched. The lover finds recognition and validity in the beloved person and the beloved person in the lover. Therefore love is the most enormous contradiction. Analytical understanding cannot understand the dialectic of love. Only dialectical reason can comprehend it. There is nothing harder than the punctuality (Punkthaf Hgkeit) of a person's self-consciousness. In love this self-consciousness is, nevertheless, negated. At the same time the lovers have their self-consciousness as something affirmative. Love is at the same time the production and resolution of its own inner contradiction. As resolution love is the socio-ethical unity which constitutes marriage and family.

6. HISTORICITY

Dialectical sociology emphasises the historicity of sexuality, erotic love, marriage and family as well as of the theological, philosophical or scientific reflection upon them.[19] The natural law thinkers of Antiquity, Middle Ages and Modernity have often looked upon marriage only according to its biological rather than its dialectical anthropological and sociological side. They often saw marriage merely as sexual or species relationship. Often to the natural law thinkers every way to the many other determinations of marriage remained closed. Sexual enlightenment turned precisely against this one-sidedly biological interpretation of marriage and stressed its other anthropological and sociological aspects.

But it was equally rude, when bourgeois enlighteners tried to comprehend marriage merely as a contract. According to bourgeois enlighteners, e.g. Kant, the mutual arbitrariness of the marriage partners comes to an agreement concerning the two individuals and their sexual parts. The bourgeois degraded marriage into the form of a mutual contractual use of the partner's sexual organs, a kind of exchange process dominated by the equivalence principle. In opposition to bourgeois enlightenment the romanticists posited marriage merely into love. Of course, love, in so far as it is feeling, allows for contingency and arbitrariness in every respect. Social morality can not have this form of accidentality. Therefore dialectical philosophy determined marriage against natural lawyers, bourgeois enlighteners and romanticists as socio-ethical love by which transitoriness, moodiness and merely subjective arbitrariness is to be superseded and unconditional mutual recognition is made possible, which may transcend even the annihilation of the one or the other partner in anamnetic solidarity.

7. ARRANGEMENT AND INCLINATION

Dialectical sociology remembers that in traditional societies marriage and family began with the arrangement by the parents.[20] The sexual and erotic inclination toward each other comes about in the persons, who are destined for the union of love by their parents, through their learning about this their destination. In the modern society, the mutual sexual and erotic inclination of the lovers as these infinitely particularised individuals constitutes the beginning of their marriage and family. The traditional world stressed universality. From this perspective, the way in which the decision to marry constitutes the beginning and has the inclination for its consequence, so that at the point of real marriage both are united, is seen to be of a higher social morality. The modern world emphasises particularity. From this view the way in which the infinite peculiarity of the lovers makes its pretense in conformity with the modern principle of free subjectivity, seems to be the more moral one. The modern sexual enlightenment, emancipation and revolution does indeed begin with the shift from parental arrangement of marriage to the sexual and erotic inclination of the lovers. This can be observed today in traditional countries, which find themselves in the process of modernisation, e.g. Saudi Arabia, Iran, Iraq, Kuwait, etc.

The dialectic of sexual enlightenment appears early in bourgeois drama and other artistic representations, long before Ch. Baudelaire, A. Strindberg and H. Ibsen.[21] In bourgeois artistic works, in which the love of the sexes constitutes the fundamental interest and all universality is forgotten, the element of penetrating frigidity, which can be found in it, is carried into the heat of sexual passion through the complete contingency and arbitrariness connected with it. This happens particularly through the fact that the artistic work represents the whole interest as resting merely on the sexes. This can be of infinite importance for the sexes, but not in and for itself. There was a price to be paid for the progressive shift from universality to particularity, from arrangement to inclination, and the price is bourgeois coldness even in matters of sexual and erotic passion.

8. SOCIAL CLASSES

According to Horkheimer, the feudal times, when the hand which used the broom on Saturday did also best caress the lord on Sunday, are indeed far removed.[22] They have disappeared to such an extent that according to the psycho-analytically enlightened bourgeois consciousness the motive of the feudal lord who marries the chamber maid lies less in his generosity than in his neurotic feeling of guilt. In the critical theorist's view such acts of the lord are pure only in bad movies. A bourgeois who thinks well of himself will not leave the marriage, not even the caressing to the maid. The bourgeois has become ambitious. He demands from the women with whom he sleeps that they have become totally, with skin and hair and everything, a luxury commodity. The declassification of the woman of the lower classes does, indeed, also concern her erotic value.

Correspondingly in the case of the man, his economic and class position belongs to his erotic potentiality. Today the American coed knows very well, if she dates a twenty-, or a fifty-thousand dollar boy, she estimates him in terms of his future earning capacity and thus is willing to exchange sexual favors for it. A man who is nothing in late capitalistic society and has nothing and does not represent any real economic chances of upward mobility has also no erotic value. The economic power can even replace the sexual power. The beautiful girl with the old man makes a fool of herself and is compromised and ridiculed only if he does not have anything. It is possible that with the consolidation of a worker's aristocracy the limit of economic power will move downward. The critical theorist combines Marx and Freud in order to assess sexuality, love and marriage in liberal and advanced capitalistic society.

9. SOCIAL PRODUCT

In Strindberg's bourgeois theater the woman appears as an evil and revengeful creature, greedy for power.[23] According to Horkheimer this negative image of the woman stems obviously from the experience of a man who is impotent in normal sexual intercourse. In such an unsatisfactory relationship the woman tends to develop in such a way as Strindberg portrays it. In the view of the critical theorist Strindberg's perspective is an example of bourgeois superficiality. Instead of going to the bottom of things, Strindberg ascribes everything to nature or better still to an infinite character structure. He ontologises the earthly woman into an eternal woman.

But Horkheimer knows only too well that to make responsible the man and his impotence for the malice of the woman means, of course, to fall into the same mistake as Strindberg himself. This is so since the impotence as well as the valuation of normal sexual intercourse as the 'rightful' form of sexual pleasure and desire is itself a social product, which changes with time. The inability of the man to perform the sexual act which the woman wishes for and which even he recognises as the measure for the masculine erotic value, is caused by the fact that he has either exhausted himself before marriage in brothel or cohabitation or that he depends in general on other forms of satisfaction. The critical theorist explains the impotence of the man together with the derogatory valuation related to it out of the history of liberal and advanced capitalistic society and his fate in its process of production and exchange. Horkheimer admits that Strindberg has mirrored well the evil woman, the impotent man and the hell which they live through together in a definite historical moment. But he has ontologised and thus eternalised the bourgeois condition as a biological one. He has mythically confused the world of nature and society. The shallower Ibsen is superior to Strindberg, because he connects the modern marital problems consciously with a transitory form of marriage and family, the bourgeois form, and thereby with capitalistic society and history.[24]

10. MARRIAGE

Horkheimer lived a long and happy marriage with his wife Maidon: She became for him the highest and she would have sacrificed her life for him.[25] But he was nevertheless aware of the fact that there takes place in this century a regress in the respect for the one and only marriage which a man or woman should enter and maintain during his or her life time and that this belongs to the dialectic of enlightenment in late capitalistic society.[26] It becomes customary to marry several times in order to reach higher and higher peak experiences. The more this happens the more declines the importance, significance and value of the individual.[27] That most divorced people remarry again one or two years after their divorce, shows to Habermas how shallow their marital relationship and individualities were in the first place.[28]

Horkheimer explains the individual's loss of value with the decline of strict monogamy out of the fact that the life of the one marital partner is held together by his or her reflection in the other partner with whom he or she lives and grows older. In advanced capitalistic society the marriage partners are very often no longer two persons who together constitute the 'I' of each of them and who make this 'I' rich through anamnesis, communicative remembrance, and enfold it in mimesis, mutual imitation and empathy. In late capitalistic society the 'I' becomes similar again to the chaotic succession of experiences. At the same time, of course, the individual is freed from the myth of marriage and family. There is progress involved here. But the liquidation of the mythical is paid for by the regression into chaos. In a certain sense the truth itself manifests itself in the process of rationalisation and enlightenment as mythical product. It looks as if man as the radical other than the animal is itself an error. While the critical theorist acknowledges the progressive aspects of sexual enlightenment and emancipation, he considers it his duty to point to the human costs involved.[29]

11. CHILDREN

According to Horkheimer it is not possible that the children whose parents have married in the age of boys and girls and soon will get divorced again, since they do not form a good household team, can learn the external and internal gestures of sensibility and reflection.[30] These children educated by those parents will finally not force themselves to do anything else than what the power of organised capitalistic society compels them to do when once the rebel leaders of the smaller societies, the motorcycle gangs, alliances and leagues come to their end. These children have not been educated and they have not learned any other motives than the brutal ones of getting ahead for any price. As far as another longing stirs in these children, which was a danger since childhood, it must be stunned and stifled through positive and negative reinforcement and further increase of brutality. In extreme exigencies this kind of education leads to that bourgeois icy coldness which makes a lie out of all the friendly gestures of the new man and the brotherly-sisterly communication community promised by religion and enlightenment alike. Sometimes the repression of longing comes forth in hate and murder. Children educated this way do no longer understand that there are other goals than those of success in empirical reality. They consider the bourgeois Christianity, which they receive on Sunday, during the week quite honestly as something completely bizarre and crazy.

12. FASHION

From its very start, the sexual enlightenment has expressed itself in fashion. In recent decades the fashion of sexual emancipation reaches from muscle shirts and miniskirts over tighter and tighter blue jeans and smaller and smaller bikinis to the body worship of the me-generation which fits together so well with the general commodity fetishism of late capitalistic society.

Benjamin describes fashion in his usual allegorical manner as the measure of time in the dialectical central station, which is death.[31] In Paris, the capital of the bourgeois world fashion opened up the dialectical transfer point between woman and commodity. Death is the long rude sales clerk of fashion. Death measures the bourgeois centuries according to the yardstick. In order to save money death makes itself the mannequin and personally leads the clearing sales. Its French name is social revolution. Sexual revolution is part of it.

For Benjamin fashion was never anything else than the woman's provocation of death. Even the woman who has terminal cancer will still dress herself 'provocatively'. In the past the woman's provocation of death has always ended with the victory of death. Fashion is the parody of the corpse. Fashion is a dialogue with the body, even with its decomposition. Once more the fashion of the newest wave of sexual enlightenment and emancipation is provocation of death: Longing for the resurrection of the body.

13. PERVERSION

According to Marcuse, originally the sexual instinct has no extraneous temporal or spatial limitations on its subject and object.[32] Sexuality is by nature polymorphous-perverse. The modern societal organisation of the sex instinct taboos defines as perversions virtually all its manifestations which do not serve or prepare for the genus act. Without the most severe restrictions, the perversions would counteract the sublimation on which the growth of culture depends. Marcuse's concept of the polymorphous perversity was one of the most important categories of the recent stage in the modern sexual enlightenment and revolution.

Horkheimer and Marcuse observe that people are always ready to become angry in late capitalistic society when the word perversion comes up.[33] They explain this by pointing to a tremendous amount of repressed wishes for other than regular genital drive satisfaction. Any victim of a despotic regime in a national security State is in bad shape when the persecutor falls upon the motive of perversion. In this case no torture is terrible enough and sufficient for the masses to extinguish the inner fire, since none is strong enough. Hitler was able to wipe out the whole left wing of his party, which demanded a revolution against the high bourgeoisie, by charging Röhm and his SA followers with homosexuality.[34]

No torture is strong enough to compensate the anti-perverts for their renunciation of perversion, which they cannot overcome. The enjoyment which the anti-perverts imagine in connection with the perversion appears to them as so superhuman that the torture and the pains with which it is requited must no longer be human. But there is almost no offense which imposes so relatively little suffering as the perversion. The exception is, of course, when force is used. But this is valid for any other business as well. As the murder attended with robbery is the non-plus-ultra of overreaching, so is rape and murder the non-plus-ultra of sexual passion. This has little or even less to do with the problem of the unusual sexual action as 'money or life' with the impirialism of multinational corporations.

Benjamin has pointed out the relativity of perversions. The horizontal position of the body had for the oldest female individuals of the human species the greatest advantages.[35] It made pregnancy easier for them. Benjamin can see this already from the girdles and bandages which pregnant women use today. Benjamin asks the question, if the upright walk did not evolve earlier with the males than the females. Then the female would at times have been the four-legged companion of the male. From this idea it is only one step to the other thought, that the frontal encounter of the two partners in sexual intercourse was originally something like a perversion. Maybe it was not at least this aberration through which the female was taught to walk upright. What once in human history was a perversion can become normal and vice versa.

In the perverse pornography of Sade and Masoch, so Horkheimer argues, cruelty can live itself out consciously as phantasy and can thus be enjoyed.[36] The really infamous action makes use of rationalisation. In times of war, which delivers such rationalisation, as well as in dictatorial States, the perversion which is master of them, grows silently. Cruelty against the enemy as well as against one's own person, can live itself out, but it can very often not be satisfied. Since the cruelty is not conscious of its sexual nature, it stretches itself, so to speak, into bad infinity. It becomes insatiable. People who are enthusiastic about wars and dictatorships are usually not able to experience the perverse enjoyment. The more they find their account in the cruelties the more greedy they become for them. Education for the ability to enjoy constitutes a decisive element in the struggle against the arriving of Future I—the totally administered society and Future II—the Thermonuclear holocaust and for the coming of Future III—the reconciled society.

14. HAPPINESS

According to Marcuse the term perversion covers sexual phenomena of essentially different origin.[37] The same taboo is placed on instinctual manifestations incompatible with high cultures and on those incompatible with repressive civilisations, especially those with monogamic genital supremacy. However, so Marcuse argues, within the historical dynamic of the sexual instinct, e.g. coprophilia and homosexuality, have a very different place and function. The same difference prevails within the same perversion. The function of sadism is not the same in a free libidinal situation and in the activity of the SS officer, who takes a Jewish woman out of the concentration camp, feeds her, sleeps with her and then gases her and then plays Chopin for the rest of the night. The inhuman, compulsive, coercive and destructive form of these perversions seem to be linked with the general perversion of human existence in a repressive civilisation.

But, according to Marcuse, the perversions have an instinctual substance distinct from these forms. This substance may very well express itself in other forms compatible with normality in high cultures. Not all component parts and stages of the instinct that have been suppressed have suffered this fate because they prevented the development of man and human kind. The purity, orderliness, cleanliness, punctuality and reproduction required by the capitalistic performance principle are not necessarily those of any mature culture. The reactivation of childhood and prehistoric wishes and attitudes is not necessarily regression and to repress them is not necessarily progress. It may very well be the opposite: Proximity to a happiness that has always been the repressed promise of a better future. According to Benjamin, origin is the goal.[38] The critical theorists agree with

Freud, when he defines happiness as the subsequent fulfillment of a prehistoric or childhood wish.[39] Eschatology is present already in archeology.

15. RECOGNITION

The critical philosophers and sociologists have a name for the solution of the human problems involved in sexual enlightenment, emancipation and revolution: *mimesis* or *imitatio*.[40] It is of Christian origin: *Imitatio Christi*.[41] For Horkheimer, Adorno and Habermas *mimesis* signifies a relationship between persons, in which the one leans upon the shoulder of the other or nestles to him or to her. One identifies with the other. One empathises with the other. *Imitatio* aims at a relationship, in which the externalisation of the one toward the example of the other does not mean the loss of himself or herself, but self-gain and self-enrichment. Shortly, *mimesis* indicates gestures of mutual, unconditional recognition, generosity, tenderness, exuberance, creative love and freedom without revenge. According to Habermas, the rational core of the mimetic impulse, ability, process and achievement can be set free when we are willing to give up in Western Civilisation the pathological philosophy of work and tools, subject-object relation, instrumental rationality in favor of a new paradigm of the philosophy of language, recognition, interaction, inter-subjectivity, practical rationality and integrate the partial functional rationality into the more embracing communicative rationality.[42]

Adorno comes very close to this paradigm change, wherever he explicates Hegel's complementary ideas of reconciliation and freedom.[43] In a comment on Eichendorff's poem, 'Beautiful Stranger', Adorno explains that the reconciliation of the lovers does not annex imperialistically what is strange and foreign.[44] The reconciled condition has its happiness in the fact that it remains in the granted nearness the distant and the different, beyond the heterogeneous and the homogeneous. Adorno describes reconciliation in terms of the undamaged, victimless intersubjectivity of the lovers. In Habermas's view such undamaged intersubjectivity comes about and maintains itself only in the reciprocity of an understanding, which rests on the mutual, free and unconditional recognition of the lovers in their being not instruments, but self-purpose.

Only once Adorno broke the critical theorists' self-imposed radicalised obedience to the Second Commandment and called the Absolute by name: Non-possessive devotion. Such devotion renders invulnerable the mutual unconditional recognition of the lovers as self-purpose even beyond the unavoidable death and destruction of the one or the other. But this can happen only in reference to an experience which makes possible the assertion of a Reality, who rescues the other who has been annihilated and thus enables the survivor to live in anamnetic solidarity with the beloved other who has been destroyed and redeemed, toward his own death and resurrection.[45] For this Reality the Judeo-Christian experience reserves the name God. To live in such anamnetic solidarity with the other who has been annihilated and rescued is not superstition or instinctual fixation. It is rather the beginning of a new, post-bourgeois form of concrete, living universality, in which the lovers are not only emancipated, but also fulfilled. Ultimately there is no unconditional, mutual recognition, mimesis, reconciliation, victimless inter-subjectivity and non-possessive devotion without resurrection and the Reality who guarantees it. If sexual enlightenment will end with the mutual instrumentalisation of the sex partners, it will have failed. If the sexual emancipation will conclude with the mutual unconditional recognition of the lovers, it will have succeeded. The battle of the sexes remains undecided.

Notes

1. M. Horkheimer *Critical Theory* (New York 1972) pp. 188–243; M. Horkheimer *Gesellschaft im Übergang* (Frankfurt a.M. 1981) pp. 162–175; A. Schmidt *Kritische Theorie, Humanismus, Aufklärung,* Stuttgart 1981) pp. 3–8, 9–24, 27–51, 95–108; A. Schmidt *Zur Idee der kritischen Theorie* (Frankfurt a.M. 1979), I–IV, pp. 7–35, 36–124, 125–136; A. Schmidt *Drei Studien über Materialismus* (Frankfurt a.M. 1979), ch. II; G. Brandt 'Ansichten kritischer Sozialforschung' in *Leviathan,* Sonderheft 4, 1981, 9–53.

2. Horkheimer *Gesellschaft,* cited in note 1, at pp. 152–160; M. Horkheimer 'E. Simmel und die Freudsche Philosophie' in *Der Stachel Freud* ed. B. Görlich, etc. (Frankfurt a.M. 1980), pp. 139–148; Th. W. Adorno 'Revidierte Psychoanalyse' in *Der Stachel Freud,* ed. B. Görlich, at pp. 119–138; H. Marcuse 'Gesellschaftliche und psychologische Repression. Die politische Aktualität Freud's' in *Der Stachel Freud,* ed. B. Görlich at pp. 186–192; A. Sohn-Rethel *Ökonomie und Klassenstruktur des deutschen Faschismus* (Frankfurt a.M. 1975) part II.

3. M. Horkheimer and Th. Adorno *Dialektik der Aufklärung* (Frankfurt a.M. 1969) IX–X; 1–7, 9–49, 88–127, 128–176, 177–217; M. Horkheimer *Eclipse of Reason* (New York 1974) ch. I, IV; M. Horkheimer *Zur Kritik der instrumentellen Vernunft* (Frankfurt a.M. 1967), pp. 335–353.

4. Habermas *Theorie des kommunikativen Handelns* (Frankfurt a.M. 1981) ch. I, II, IV.

5. M. Horkheimer *Zur Kritik des kommunikativen Handelns* pp. 63–92.

6. Horkheimer *Eclipse of Reason,* ch. I, II, III; Th. W. Adorno, etc. *Der Positivismusstreit in der deutschen Soziologie* (Darmstadt 1980) pp. 7–80, 81–102, 125–144, 155–192, 235–266; Horkheimer *Gesellschaft im Übergang* pp. 162–175; M. Horkheimer *Die Sehnsucht nach dem ganz Anderen* (Hamburg 1970) pp. 60–61; M. Horkheimer *Notizen 1950–1969 und Dämmerung* (Frankfurt a.M. 1974) pp. 101–104, 116–117.

7. Habermas *Theorie des kommunikativen Handelns* pp. 504–505.

8. Horkheimer *Die Sehnsucht nach dem ganz Anderen* pp. 66–67; Th. W. Adorno/E. Kogon 'Offenbarung oder autonome Vernunft' in *Frankfurter Hefte* 13/6 (June 1958), 397–398; W. Benjamin *Schriften I* (Frankfurt a.M. 1950) p. 494; H. Marcuse *Eros and Civilization* (New York 1962) p. 66.

9. J. Habermas *Theory and Praxis* (Boston 1973) ch. 6; Habermas *Theorie der kommunikativen Handelns* ch. VIII, esp. 383, ch. IX; Habermas *Politik, Kunst, Religion* (Stuttgart 1978) pp. 127–142; Habermas 'Tod in Jerusalem' in *Merkur* 4/36 (April 1982), 438–440; Horkheimer *Gesellschaft im Übergang* pp. 162–175; Adorno/Kogon, the article cited in note 8, 397–402; R. J. Siebert *Horkheimer's Critical Sociology of Religion: The Relative and the Transcendent* (Washington, D.C. 1979) ch. I, III, IV, V, VI, VIII.

10. Horkheimer *Die Sehnsucht nach dem ganz Anderen* pp. 72–75.

11. Horkheimer *Gesellschaft im Übergang* pp. 162–175; Horkheimer *Die Sehnsucht nach dem ganz Anderen* pp. 54–89; Th. W. Adorno *Minima Moralia* (Frankfurt a.M. 1980) pp. 333–334; W. Benjamin *Reflections* (New York 1978) pp. 312–313; W. Benjamin *Illuminations* (New York 1976) pp. 253–264.

12. Horkheimer *Zur Kritik der instrumentellen Vernunft* p. 148.

13. *Ibid.* p. 236.

14. M. Horkheimer *Studien über Autorität und Familie* (Paris 1936); E. Fromm *The Dogma of Christ* (New York 1963) pp. 203–212; E. Fromm *The Art of Loving* (New York 1956) pp. 83–106; Marcuse *Eros and Civilization* parts 1 and 2, 217–251; H. Marcuse *Negations* (Boston 1969) ch. VII; H. Marcuse *Five Lectures* (Boston 1970) ch. I, II, III; W. Benjamin *Das Passagen-Werk* (Frankfurt a.M. 1983) pp. 612–642, 997–1000; R. J. Siebert *Hegel's Concept of Marriage and Family: The Origin of Subjective Freedom* (Washington, D.C. 1979) ch. 25–31.

15. Schmidt *Kritische Theorie, Humanismus, Aufklärung* pp. 95–108; G. W. F. Hegel *System der Philosophie* (Stuttgart-Bad Cannstatt 1965) II, pp. 66–722.

16. *Ibid.*

17. G. W. F. Hegel *System der Philosophie* (Stuttgart-Bad Cannstatt 1965) p. 109.

18. G. W. F. Hegel *Grundlinien der Philosophie des Rechts* (Stuttgart-Bad Cannstatt 1964)

pp. 237–260. (SW 7); Horkheimer *Notizen, 1950–1969 und Dämmerung* pp. 5–8, 21–22, 41, 59, 83, 138–139, 142–144, 168–169, 181, 187–188, 203–204; Marcuse *Negations* ch. VII; Fromm *The Art of Loving* ch. I–IV; Siebert *Hegel's Concept of Marriage and the Family* ch. 9–24.

19. SW 7, 239–241; Horkheimer *Notizen 1950–1969 und Dämmerung* pp. 240, 292–293, 142–144, 148, 197–198, 307–308, 47–48; Marcuse *Negations* ch. VII.

20. SW 7, 240–241.

21. *Ibid.*; Ch. Baudelaire *Flowers of Evil* (New York 1936) pp. 3–4, 7–9, 63–67, 81–84, 97–103, 143–146; Benjamin *Das Passagen Werk* pp. 301–489; A. Strindberg *The Chamber Plays* (New York 1962) vii–xxiv; H. Ibsen *When we dead awaken and three other plays* (Garden City, New York 1960) xiii–xiv, 3–14.

22. Horkheimer *Notizen 1950–1969 und Dämmerung* p. 240.

23. *Ibid.* pp. 292–293; Strindberg *The Chamber Plays* pp. 1–201.

24. Horkheimer *Notizen 1950–1969 und Dämmerung* p. 240; Ibsen *When we dead awaken* pp. 1–108, 109–216, 311–381.

25. Horkheimer *Die Sehnsucht nach dem ganz Anderen* p. 73.

26. Horkheimer *Notizen 1950–1969 und Dämmerung* pp. 148, 142–144.

27. *Ibid.*; Horkheimer *Eclipse of Reason* ch. 4.

28. J. Habermas *Legitimation Crisis* (Boston 1975) part III, ch. 4.

29. Horkheimer *Die Sehnsucht nach dem ganz Anderen* pp. 54–89, esp. 73–75.

30. Horkheimer *Notizen 1950–1969 und Dämmerung* pp. 59, 296–297, 339, 43.

31. Benjamin *Das Passagen Werk* pp. 997, 1000, 1054–1055.

32. Marcuse *Eros and Civilisation* p. 44.

33. *Ibid.* pp. 44–45; Horkheimer *Notizen 1950–1969 und Dämmerung* pp. 30, 15, 195–196.

34. Sohn-Rethel *Ökonomie und Klassenstruktur der deutschen Faschismus* pp. 200–210.

35. Benjamin *Das Passagen Werk* pp. 131–132.

36. Horkheimer *Notizen 1950–1969 und Dämmerung* pp. 195–196; Horkheimer/Adorno, *Dialektik der Aufklärung* pp. 88–127.

37. Marcuse *Eros and Civilisation* pp. 185–196.

38. Benjamin *Illuminations* p. 261.

39. E. Jones *The Life and Work of S. Freud* (New York 1953) I, p. 330.

40. Habermas *Theorie der kommunikativen Handelns* pp. 512–513, 518, 522–525.

41. *Ibid.*; Horkheimer *Notizen 1950–1969 und Dämmerung* pp. 170–171.

42. Habermas *Theorie der kommunikativen Handelns* pp. 522–523; J. Habermas *Theory and Praxis* (Boston 1971) ch. 4; G. W. F. Hegel *Jenaer Systementwürfe I* (Hamburg 1975) pp. 282–296, 296–300, 301–306, 307–315; G. W. F. Hegel *Jenaer Systementwürfe III* (Hamburg 1976) pp. 185–201, 202–209, 209–223, 233–236.

43. Habermas *Theorie der kommunikativen Handelns* pp. 518–523.

44. T. W. Adorno *Gesammelte Schriften* (Frankfurt a.M. 1973), vol. VI, pp. 6, 192.

45. H. Peukert *Wissenschaftstheorie-Handlungstheorie-Fundamentale Theologie* (Düsseldorf 1976), part III, esp. 289–302; E. Arens *Kommunikative Handlungen* (Düsseldorf 1982) part IV, esp. pp. 374–385.

D

PART II

Consequences and Problems

Susan Hanks

The Sexual Revolution and Violence Against Women: The Boundary Between Liberation and Exploitation

TO THE READER: Men's sexual violence against women is probably not a topic a reader approaches with great delight. Rather, it is likely the reader may resist thinking about violence toward women. This resistance is predictable. One essential ingredient to Western society's perpetuation of violence against women is the taboo surrounding it. This taboo does not, of course, prohibit men from acting violently towards women—it only prohibits men and women from acknowledging it. Hence, if the reader is resistant, the taboo is effective. It is the author's hope that the reader will master his/her resistance, break the taboo, and continue reading.

One of the results of the sexual revolution that has occurred in Western societies over the last several decades has been the separation of questions of sexual mores from questions of personal morality. This distinction has allowed men and women the freedom necessary to creatively explore and educate themselves about healthy human sexuality without the intrusions of social sanctions. In this evolutionary process, traditional boundaries of sexual morality were inevitably crossed. As a consequence, the line between one person's liberation and another person's exploitation sometimes became unclear. This essay will explore men's sexual violence towards women as a crossing of the boundary between liberation and exploitation. Stranger rape, spousal rape, incest and pornography will be used to exemplify the age old phenomenon of violence against women. Issues to be explored include: How has the banner of the sexual revolution, with its promise to liberate, been exploited to rationalise men's violence against women? How has the patriarchal bias inherent in gender role socialisation contributed to the occurrence of, and denial of, violence against women? What is the collective moral responsibility of men and women in disarming human relationships?

1. THE RE-EVOLUTION OF SEXUAL MORES

The sexual revolution of the last few decades ushered in new cultural mores about sexuality and male/female relationships. The pleasures of the body were allegedly rediscovered and sanctioned. Attitudes about virginity, monogamy, orgasm, sexual censorship in the media, homosexuality, bi-sexuality and auto-sexuality were examined. Couples experimented with 'open marriage' and 'free love'. With the advent of The Pill, men and women attained control over their reproductive selves. Recreational sexual activity could be distinguished from procreational sexual activity. The impact on human behaviour was far reaching.

The dark side of the revolution emerged with the depersonalisation and trivialisation of sexual activity. 'It' became something you 'have' or 'do' or 'get'. 'It' became a way of selling things—like cigarettes, automobiles or clothing. The person with whom one was 'having it' sometimes became lost. This phenomenon was particularly apparent in the popularisation of the 'Playboy Ethic' and the mushrooming of the production of pornography into a multi-million dollar business. Marketing the image of women, and more recently of children, as sex objects ('chicks' or 'bunnies') to be utilised for male sexual pleasures became profitable. Developing authentic female/male relationships characterised by tenderness, intimacy and mutuality remained as elusive as always, in spite of new found sexual freedoms.

2. THE PROCESS OF PATRIARCHAL SOCIALISATION

Western society's changing sexual mores evolved under the umbrella of the overall dominant culture. The patriarchal nature of the dominant culture has a profound effect on the culture's view of women, men and heterosexual relationships. It is important to understand the patriarchal bias in order to understand the dynamics of male violence towards women.

(a) The patriarchal bias

The patriarchal bias influencing the social and personal development of men and women is subtle, pervasive and often unrecognised. Patriarchal values are smoothly integrated into our gender role socialisation process. (That is, the process by which boys and girls learn about which behaviours, attitudes, and feelings are appropriate for members of their own sex, and which are appropriate for, and about, members of the opposite sex). This integration is often so successful that we have difficulty distinguishing between behaviour that is biologically innate versus behaviour that is learned in the culture. (This dynamic is evident in the current cultural debate of whether or not men's violence is innate versus learned).

(b) Devaluing the feminine

As a patriarchal culture, Western society teaches men and women that the male (and by implication all that is masculine) is the norm or standard to which all else is compared. That which is other than male is deviant from the norm and, therefore, inferior. Males, and masculine qualities, are valued; while females, and feminine qualities, are devalued. In the patriarchal scheme, there is no concept of different but equal.

(c) The disadvantaged female

Thanks to the recent resurgence of feminist scholarship, our consciousness has been raised about the reality of the patriarchal culture's devaluation of women (and, by implication, the feminine) and its effect on the lives of women. In addition to stranger and spousal rape, pornography and incest (to be discussed later), examples in the history of the United States are abundant. Less than 100 years ago a woman could neither vote, hold public office, attain a higher education, nor keep her name, money or property after marriage. Wife battery was legalised by statute which allowed men to 'chastise' their wives as long as they did not use a 'stick larger than their thumb'. (Hence, the colloquial expression 'rule of thumb'.)[1] The recognition of violence towards women was virtually suppressed on a cultural level. When women from the Women's Christian Temperance Union (WCTU) attempted to elevate wife battery to the level of a social problem related to alcohol abuse, they were eventually discounted as tee-totalers and prudes.[2]

From a psychological perspective, Freud supplies us with a window into the collective unconscious mental life of the patriarchy by his definition of women as the secondary sex inclined to masochism, intellectual inferiority, narcissism, hysteria and envy.[3] Recently, the defeat of the Equal Rights Amendment in the United States legitimised the same type of discrimination against a woman based on her sex, that is already outlawed based on her race or religion.

(d) The disadvantaged male

The impact of the patriarchy's devaluation of the feminine on men's lives in Western society is much harder to pinpoint, less well documented, but none-the-less potent. At first glance, men appear less disadvantaged than women. The culture promotes the illusion that men themselves are in control of their own gender role socialisation. Many men who seemingly benefit from their 'masculine privilege' either seem oblivious to its restraints and disadvantages—or rationalise the exercising of their 'privilege' as a legitimate compensation for the very burdens it creates. Some men may just be aware of the disadvantages of their 'privilege', e.g. those suffering the stress inherent in being the middle class sole-bread-winner/head-of-household. Other men may feel deprived of the rewards of their 'masculine privilege', i.e. money, status and power, and assert their 'privilege' in the only legitimate arena the culture leaves open to them—in the domination and subjugation of 'their' women through violence.

Literature in the field of domestic violence is beginning to speak of the disadvantages of the patriarchal culture to men. The question being researched in that field is: Why do men, who are supposedly so advantaged, beat, rape, humiliate, or degrade women—often women who are their wives, lovers or daughters—often women whom they love and upon whom they depend. There are numerous ways to answer this question.

One explanation is related to the psychological and social violence men experience in the process of male gender role socialisation. The patriarchal culture, which rewards masculine traits and devalues feminine traits, harshly shames and demeans little boys into disassociating from their feminine qualities. The ultimate insult for a little boy is to be called a 'sissy'.[4] For little boys, only a disavowal of wishes to be nurturant, emotionally expressive, dependent and submissive, along with a denial of feelings of fear, sadness, weakness and confusion is tolerated. For men, acknowledging feelings or wishes on this prohibited list results in the loss of respect by self and others. A man's need to purge himself of his feminine qualities are manifest both in his violence towards women and in his homophobic behavior towards homosexual men.[5]

Almost all men do in fact experience feelings and wishes defined as feminine. However, men who are violent towards women may be so well socialised that they are psychologically incapable of conscious awareness of these prohibited feelings. When they do experience these feelings, even on an unconscious level, men are psychologically incapable of tolerating them. By projecting the intolerable feelings onto devalued women, men can assert dominion and control over the women and, hence, over the feelings through physical assault.[6]

Another component of male gender role socialisation contributing to violence towards women lies in the psychological process of attachment and separation little boys experience. According to standard psychological theory, the attachment a child forms with a primary caretaking person is essential to healthy psychological development. In Western societies, the primary caretaker of young children is usually the mother. In the process of successful gender development in a patriarchal culture, little boys must not only disavow their feminine feelings and wishes but also give up their attachment to the primary nurturing female. In essence, the little boys are expected to relinquish their attachment to a highly valued love object. The patriarchal culture discounts the little boy's loss by discounting or devaluing that which he is losing. (How can little boys regret losing something which had no value anyway?) Many boys emerge from this process as men who are threatened by attachment to others, who lose the ability to be emphatic with others and who fear intimacy in relationships.[7] Interestingly enough, these are three essential ingredients in the personality of men who are violent.

Violence towards the feminine in a patriarchal culture may in fact be displaced rage against the patriarchy which forced little boys to abandon something they highly valued. However, it is culturally more acceptable to act out this rage against women, who are allowed to maintain feminine qualities disavowed by boys, than to rage against the patriarchy.

The disadvantages of patriarchal gender role socialisation was the unspoken theme evident in the rise of the 'Playboy Ethic'. Playboy magazine, first published in 1953, served as the pop manifesto advocating male revolt against 'grey flannel conformity' and the bondage of the bread winner ethic.[8] Unfortunately, the hostility was not directed toward the process of patriarchal gender role socialisation (which, after all, is a real but none-the-less abstract concept) but against women (who are available and real). Marriage and fatherhood, basic interpersonal activities whose success requires personality development in the areas of empathy, intimacy and attachment, were not surprisingly recast as oppressive traps stultifying to personal growth.[9] Hostility towards women was evident not only in its derision of respect and nurturance in human relationships but also in its pioneering of the mass marketing of the fantasy model of sexuality and the sexual objectification of women and children. The phenomenal financial success of the magazine and the boom in the pornography business that followed is evidence of the powerful appeal its message has had to the collective cultural unconscious of men in Western society.

It could be that men who violently act out the culture's devaluation of the feminine through sexual violence towards women are perhaps the patriarchy's strongest adherents. They have internalised their gender lessons well.

3. THE POLARISATION OF MEN AND WOMEN

Men and women absorb from their environment both factual information, cultural norms and numerous myths concerning male-female relationships. A preponderance of information is learned through the media—from relatively benign to erotic or pornographic television programmes, films, books and magazines. As the intent of the media is usually other than educational, the models we receive of men and women's relationships, particularly in the arena of sexuality, are often distorted, sometimes superhuman, and rarely, if ever, reality based.

For example, one seemingly benign classic movie most children see projected gender role stereotypes into an already potent fairytale. The 1938 Disney movie 'Snow White and the Seven Dwarfs' presents us with the female models of the innocent virgin versus the wicked witch and subtly injects men's fear of the domination of women into the plot. In the movie, the dwarf Grumpy is heard to warn the other dwarfs that Snow White will '. . . make a sissy out of you' and '. . . give 'em [women] an inch and they'll take a mile'. When Grumpy is asked by Dopey what he meant by 'wiles' when he said 'females is [sic] full of wicked wiles', Grumpy's response is 'I don't know, but I'm ag'in 'em'. Grumpy was obviously well socialised.

Unfortunately, women themselves are not exempt from promoting these gender role stereotypes. *Total Woman* by Marabel Morgan (the widely sold 1973 publication) teaches women techniques of how to use their alleged female wiles to counter their domination by men by manipulating and controlling men without their knowledge. This book presented a view of women as childlike, subordinate and manipulative. Unfortunately, just what Grumpy has suspected. Apparently, Ms. Morgan and her followers were also well socialised by the patriarchy.

Other myths, more subtle, particularly around the area of sexuality, have contributed to the polarisation of men and women. Supposedly, girls no longer believe that boys will lose respect for them once they've 'done it', and, supposedly, boys will not. Boys are no longer 'out after just one thing'. Women are no longer considered 'vessels of sin' or 'devil's gateways'. Men are no longer struggling with concupiscence as St. Augustine did so many centuries ago.

Supposedly, the sexual revolution has helped to dispel many of these myths by encouraging men and women to become educated about their own and their partner's reality based needs. Hopefully, this process will minimize the culturally acquired projections, assumptions and distortions many men and women have of each other. Dispelling these myths will minimise the polarisation of men and women in the patriarchal culture which lays the foundation for violence against women.

4. LINKING SEX AND VIOLENCE

Although the role model of the virgin martyr (whose inspirational value rested in being beautiful, young, chaste and dead) is allegedly obsolete, the patriarchal culture conveys to women in many ways the danger that can befall them because of their sex and sexuality. A song popularised by The Beatles in the 1960s, 'Run for Your Life', warns women that men prefer their women dead to disloyal.

Violence against women is more than a fabrication in the minds of men or a fantasy portrayed in the media. Men who rape women, men who batter and rape their wives and lovers, men who create and finance pornography, men who sexually abuse their daughters are all too real. Tragically, so also are the women and girls who are raped, battered, violated and demeaned.

The rate of occurrence of violence against women remains unclear. Accurate statistical records are recent events. According to the Federal Bureau of Investigation in the United States, the crimes of rape, incest and wife battery all vie for the dubious distinction of being the most underreported crimes. What is widely accepted is that these crimes occur much more often than reported.

(a) Stranger rape

Rape serves the function of expressing and perpetuating male domination of women (and the feminine qualities they personify) by violence. Every successfully acculturated woman grows up to fear rape (it would be a denial of the reality not to fear it) and, by implication, to fear men. A rape free society would be one in which women could move freely without the fear of men. Even though all men do not rape, many men do. Recent research data shows that a woman has a 46% chance of being a victim of completed or attempted rape at some point in her life.[10] There is no comparable data available related to the probability a man will rape in his lifetime, or how many times he will rape. Men who rape are not necessarily mentally disordered. For instance, mass rape in war is a common phenomenon by both the occupying and liberating forces.[11]

Rape is an act of aggression and violence, not a sexual act. The intent is to humiliate and terrorise the victim, never to satisfy her. Victims are chosen for their sex, not for their sex appeal. Victims can be any age, young children or fragile seniors. Rape can occur in any location, although it most frequently occurs on the street, in the victim's home or car.[12]

(b) Spousal rape

The relationship between the assailant and the victim is a major component in how a patriarchal society defines rape, whether rape becomes a crime, and whether the victim is blamed or assisted. Anonymity between the victim and rapist is often a prerequisite for defining rape. Hence, rape in marriage is commonly considered a contradiction in terms. This notion is reflected in American criminal statutes which commonly define rape as 'forced sexual intercourse with a female *not the wife* of the perpetrator'[13] (emphasis added). Defining forced sex in marriage as rape challenges the patriarchal view of wives as husbands' property (men can't steal something that belongs to them), and the 'wifely duty' being one of total sexual availability (so only negligent wives can be forced). Hence, the 'marital exemption' applies a legal double standard which decriminalises behaviour between spouses that would be considered criminal between strangers.

Marital rape is a common form of the physical and psychological violence over two million battered wives endure in America each year.[14] Mounting evidence indicates that twice as many women are raped by their husbands each year than by strangers. Marital rape can be even more psychologically traumatic for the victim who has to live with her rapist and who is intimately violated by the person who is supposed to love her. Like stranger rape, spousal rape is an expression of power and hostility, not sexuality. Men who rape their wives do so less because of sexual rejection than in response to the feelings that sexual rejection produce in them.[15]

(c) Incest

The cultural taboo against incest (sexual relations between children and older family members), like that against all forms of violence against women, is apparently not in the doing of it but in the acknowledging of it. Incest follows the general pattern of child sexual abuse, with the majority of victims being female and the majority of assailants being male. The actual rate of occurrence is unknown. It has been conservatively estimated that about one million American women are survivors of incestuous relationships with their fathers.[16]

Incest is rape in the sense that it is a coerced sexual relationship. However, because of the relationship with the assailant and the victim's seeming compliance, it is not always defined by society as rape. The violence of incest is not necessarily the physical sexual behaviour itself but the exploitation of the power differential inherent in the parent-child relationship. Little girls, as dependent children, are compelled to obey, to collude in the secrecy of the behaviour, and to submit themselves to the domination of the father. Incest is a significant trauma for female children and may have long-lasting deleterious effects on their lives.[17]

(d) Pornography

Pornography is differentiated from sexually explicit erotic or educational material in that it has as its distinguishing characteristic the degrading or demeaning portrayal of human beings, especially women. Pornography, whether verbal or pictorial, is the propaganda which promotes the act of rape.[18]

Under the rhetoric of sexual liberation and freedom of the press, pornography explicitly links sex and violence. Women are raped, tortured, mutilated, bound, etc., as a way of sexually stimulating male characters. The violence of these acts is trivialised by presenting women as enjoying being abused.

This violence has escalated in recent years to the production of 'snuff' films—so called because the actresses are actually murdered in front of the camera in order to allegedly provide sexual stimulation for the viewers.

'Kiddy Porn' is the latest fashion on the pornography circuits—a mere substitution of the 'real thing' for women who have long been infantilised in portrayals of 'little girls' who idolise 'big men'. The sexual linking of adult males with little girls distorts situations of child sexual abuse portraying them as positive experiences. The viewer is led to believe that adult-child sexual activity can be a neutral or even positive experience for the child. This is a direct attack on the culturally imposed incest taboo.[19]

5. A QUESTION OF HARM

With the separation of cultural mores from questions of morality, the sexual revolution brought into question long-standing restrictions on sexual behaviour in Western society. Society in general became more accepting of sexual behaviours that were formerly considered deviant or inappropriate, if not immoral. In the process of arriving at more liberated social attitudes and norms, society became appropriately cautious in standing in judgment over sexual behaviours.

This trend has made it difficult for proponents of sexual liberation, particularly in a patriarchal culture, to critically assess the problem of male violence against women. The sexual aspects become confused with the violent aspects. Lines between liberation and exploitation become blurred. For instance, civil libertarians recoil at the prospect of linking pornography and rape because it might lead to censorship in the media. Marriage traditionalists, having internalised patriarchal values well, puzzle over the issue of spousal rape because they view women as precipitating their own assault by 'withholding' husbands' sexual rights. Proponents of child sexual liberation view the incest taboo as outdated and as a restriction of children's rights to sexual satisfaction.

Persons of both liberal and conservative persuasions are reluctant to encourage social intervention in the 'sanctity of the family'. Many are reluctant to make a social or public issue out of what is considered to be a private or family affair. In addition, anyone venturing to suggest a re-imposing of social limits on what is seen as sexual behaviour risks being labelled reactionary if not prudish.

Fortunately for society, the sexual revolution has not been the only revolution occurring in Western society in the last few decades. A resurgence of the women's liberation movement brought with it a critical look at the issues of stranger rape, spousal rape, pornography and incest from a non-patriarchal, feminist perspective. The creation of shelters for battered women and of support services for rape victims and survivors of incest shattered the social taboo of secrecy surrounding violence against women. The feminist research in the social sciences reminded society that the behaviour of the rapist, pornographer and incestuous father is not sexual but violent. Violence was shown to be harmful to the victim. Therefore, the question of harm and, hence, of morality can no longer be overlooked.

The moral question at hand is not whether certain sexual behaviours are wrong or right but whether society can morally justify continuing to deny the knowledge that patriarchal oppression of both men and women leads to the rape, humiliation and exploitation of women. Men and women who collude with the patriarchy and suppress this knowledge are indirectly morally responsible for the perpetuation of violence against women.

6. NEEDED: A DISARMAMENT OF THE HEART

The sexual revolution cannot successfully occur unless accompanied by a gender role revolution. A rape free, pornography free, incest free culture would be one in which women no longer feared men and men no longer needed women to fear them. This revolution would be most radical and far reaching in that it would free human relationships from the oppression of patriarchal values. The need to maintain power in human relationships through patriarchal dynamics of domination and subordination would be obsolete. Power would be utilised not to control but to create. Utilising the gift of free will unique to the human species to move beyond retaliatory rage, men and women could collaborate in changing what appears to be our collective destiny of patriarchally inspired nuclear self destruction. Ending men's violence against women is the first step in disarming our hearts, our homes and our relationships and one step closer to disarming The Bomb. We and our children deserve no less.

Notes

1. R. Emerson Dobash-Russell Dobash *Violence Against Wives: A Case Against the Patriarchy* (New York 1979).

2. Elizabeth Pleck 'Feminist Responses to "Crimes Against Women," 1868–1896' *Signs: Journal of Women in Culture and Society* (1983) 8(3) 450–470.

3. Judith Van Herik 'The Feminist Critique of Classical Psychoanalysis' *Concilium: The Challenge of Psychology to Faith* (1982) pp. 83–86.

4. Stan Taubman 'Beyond the Bravado: Male Sex-Role Acquisition and Domestic Violence' (Manuscript under submission for publication) (Berkeley, CA. 1983).

5. See Taubman, the work cited in note 4; Bernie Zilbergeld *Male Sexuality* (New York 1978); Personal communication, Daniel Sonkin, PhD, Berkeley, CA., July 1983.

6. Observations based on the author's clinical experience as a psychotherapist working with situations of family violence.

7. Carol Gilligan *In A Different Voice* (Cambridge, MA. 1982). Nancy Chodorow *The Reproduction of Mothering* (Berkeley 1978).

8. Barbara Ehrenreich *The Hearts of Men: American Dream and the Flight from Commitment* (New York 1983).

9. Susan Brownmiller *Against Our Will/Men, Women and Rape* (New York 1975).

10. Diane E. H. Russell and Nancy Howell 'The Prevalence of Rape in the United States Revisited' *Signs: Journal of Women in Culture and Society* (1983) 8(4) 688–695.

11. Brownmiller, the work cited in note 9, Robin Morgan 'Theory and Practice: Pornography and Rape' *Take Back the Night/Women on Pornography* ed. Laura Lederer (New York 1980).

12. Brownmiller, the work cited in note 9.

13. Irene Hanson Frieze 'Investigating the Causes and Consequences of Marital Rape' *Signs: Journal of Women in Culture and Society* (1983) 8(3) 532–553; Zak Mettger 'A Case of Rape: Forced Sex in Marriage' *Response to Family Violence* (1982) 5(2).

14. Del Martin *Battered Wives* (San Francisco 1975); *The Social Causes of Husband-Wife Violence* eds. Murray Straus and Gerald Hotaling, (Minneapolis 1980); Lenore Walker *The Battered Woman* (New York 1979).

15. Frieze, the article cited in note 13, Mettger, the article cited in the same note.

16. Judith Herman *Father Daughter Incest* (Cambridge, Ma. 1981).

17. *Ibid.*

18. Diane E. H. Russell 'Pornography and Violence: What Does the New Research Say?' *Take Back the Night/Women on Pornography* ed. Laura Lederer (New York 1980); Morgan, the article cited in note 11.

19. Laura Lederer 'Playboy Isn't Playing' *Take Back the Night/Women on Pornography* ed. Laura Lederer (New York 1980).

Antonio Hortelano

The Sexual Revolution and the Family

IN THE West the family is passing through a period of critical change. In less than a hundred years the Western world family has ceased to be rural and patriarchal and rapidly become urban and nuclear. And while this phenomenon is still barely taking shape, we already feel the urgent need to do something about the serious botch-up made by the industrial age in the matter of the family and in much else, for example, urbanism. And, even more surprisingly, we find that the Western world is not just striving to resolve certain structural problems of the urban nuclear family, but beginning to come up with utopias. Groups of pioneers are trying out new models of the family which would suit the now imminent post-industrial age. Perhaps new generations do not want to be taken by surprise in the matter of the family, as were the makers of the industrial revolution, who had to improvise a model of the city and of the family as they went along, with the result that it emerged weedy and weak. The impression of a 'botch-up' given by the urban nuclear family today, in spite of all its indisputable successes, may help us considerably to make things better for the family of the future. In this serious crisis of the Western family the sexual revolution has been very, although not exclusively, important.

1. THE SEXUAL REVOLUTION

The social and ethical channelling of sexuality goes back to very remote times. From ancient times people have been aware that it was necessary to channel the impetuous force of sexuality. With 'homo sapiens' the natural control of sexuality—alternating periods of heat and rest—that exists in animals disappeared. It was found necessary to replace it with a form of cultural control. But even in very ancient times and among primitive peoples, metaphysical and religious notions frequently converted this control into a morbid dualism. God is good. Evil comes from the adversary. God is light. Evil is darkness. Light is spirit. Flesh is darkness. Therefore everything related directly to the body is dark, ugly and ultimately evil. Hence the socio-cultural discrediting of sex and manual labour.

Christianity reacted energetically against the extremes of dualism: condemnation of the Encratists of Corinth (St Paul), the Manichees (St Augustine), the Albigensians (St Thomas) and finally of the Jansenists, who were influenced by Calvinism (St Alphonsus). However despite all this, Christianity did not succeed in freeing itself totally from the dualist intoxication. This largely explains the modern sexual revolution.

(a) Freud—Reich—Marcuse

Freud brought out the importance of the 'libido' in the human psyche. The love instinct (life), together with the instinct of aggression (death) accepted later by Freud through pressure from Adler and the fact of the Great War, are fundamental to the understanding of the human unconscious and conscious world. Certainly, according to Freud, culture requires the repression of sexuality. This is the social cost we have to pay to live in a civilised manner. But this control must be conscious and not unconscious. Unconscious repression is the cause of neurosis.

Reich, Freud's disciple, broke with the master precisely on this issue of 'sexual politics'. Certainly, according to Reich, some cultures can only exist on a basis of sexual repression, but societies have existed which did not practise any kind of sexual repression. This revolution is not easy, Reich said, but it is possible.

Marcuse on the crest of the revolutionary fervour of '68 held that Western culture has created the conditions for a non-repressive civilisation. He re-stated Freudian theory in opposition to E. Fromm, K. Horney, and H. Stack Sullivan and other neo-Freudians, who according to Marcuse, had abandoned some of the most important discoveries made by psychoanalytic theory.

(b) The spread of the sexual revolution in the west

The United States has been regarded as the home of liberty. This, in spite of a certain atavistic puritanism in the North American people, explains why the sexual revolution found in the US a more favourable climate in which to take root than in other countries. The characteristic North American forms of the sexual revolution were the 'modular family' and the hippy phenomenon.

Many people thought of Scandinavia as the paradise of the sexual revolution. One of the most insistent manifestations of sexual freedom in Scandinavia has been the appearance in recent years of sexual communes which have usually ended in collapse.

The history of the sexual revolution in the Soviet Union is disconcerting. The socialisation of the family in the USSR met with far more difficulties in fact than the socialisation of the means of production. Socialising the home is not the same for the worker as socialising industry. This was true despite the fact that at the beginning the sexual revolution met with great enthusiasm in the USSR. For the first time in Western history, a whole people tried to revise radically and consciously its family base. Discussions on the subject began with the revolution, increased in the succeeding years but from 1923 onwards died down until they stopped altogether and gave way to a conservative reaction from the years 1933–35 when Stalinism was in full flood. Perhaps the main cause of this backwards march in the Russian sexual revolution was the theoretical poverty of marxism in the matter of the family.

In the rest of the Western world the movement for sexual liberation has been spreading gradually and acquiring more polemical and strident tones in the more puritan countries like England and Holland, where sexual liberation has come up against the sturdy resistance of the Victorian spirit and Calvinism respectively. In Spain repression was never very serious, as may be seen from the great myths created by Spanish literature such as 'La Celestina' and 'Don Juan'.

2. FROM PURITAN REPRESSION TO EROTIC CONSUMERISM

Unfortunately, the sexual revolution, which could have meant an authentic liberation and partly was, frequently deteriorated into an erotic consumerism. In fact it is one thing to try to free ourselves from sexual taboos or irrational prohibitive obsessions and quite a different thing to be obsessed with the idea that the only important and decisive thing in men's lives is sexuality, especially when it becomes an article for consumption (prostitution) or, at least, an object of commercial propaganda.

Recently a form of post-revolutionary neo-puritanism has arisen, as if many people, while not denying the positive achievements of sexual liberation, were beginning to realise that in order to achieve anything important in life, they needed to be hard and to channel the overflowing force of sexuality.

3. IMPACT ON THE WESTERN FAMILY

The sexual revolution has had an important impact on the Western family.

(a) Diffuse sexuality

The irruption of women into the outside world as a result of their promotion as persons, partly through the two world wars which forced rulers to rely on them to do the work the fighting men could not do, has led to a situation in which men and women are together everywhere from childhood onwards. This has led to great developments in the relations between men and women beyond strict genitality. It has given rise to a kind of diffuse sexuality allowing men and women rich possibilities of interrelating, but which, especially at the beginning, led to not a few personal and family problems.

(b) Effect of the sexual explosion on the family as an institution

The sexual revolution and the present crisis in the urban nuclear family has led to a radical questioning of the institutional bases of the traditional family.

(i) *Premarital relations*

It is not easy for young people today to practise continence before marriage. On the one hand, they find that society forces them to delay marriage for economic reasons for a long time after they have reached biological and psychological maturity. On the other hand, they are bombarded by the media, which have changed from repressive puritan obsession to another kind of obsession with sexual consumption.

(ii) *Relations outside marriage*

There is no doubt that today a form of neo-polygamy is coming into being. The irruption of women into the world—they used to be shut away—the democratisation of love as a free choice, the acceleration of consumption and what is on offer in a society of deafening pluralism have all favoured this new polygamy, which is sometimes experienced as a compensation for a deteriorating marriage and sometimes as an opening towards a non-conventional future of marriage, although the results of this latter claim do not in general appear to be very satisfactory.

(iii) *Divorce*

There have always been marital breakdowns, but today these are reaching a worrying level. Certain factors have contributed to this: the uprooting of the rural population, the crisis of institutions in general and marriage in particular, the lengthening of the life expectancy of marriage, which is now more than fifty years, the psychological frailty of people left to their own devices in a world tormented and tense among extremist utopias and bloody critical analyses.

Although people whose marriages have broken down cannot be prevented from seeking to escape from neurosis-producing solitude, nevertheless the consequences are very serious for the children, the parties concerned and society in general, when people are condemned to live with the anxious and systematic doubt about whether they can count on their partner forever, come what may.

The only way of radically overcoming the permanent temptation to existential insecurity is to be able to count on someone prepared, in any cirumstances, to give their life for you and vice versa.

(iv) *Responsible parenthood*

The sexual revolution has brought about an important change in what men and women seek from marriage. In the past the important and decisive thing was to have children. They were necessary for the survival of the human race and to insure the parents' old age. Today the world is overpopulated, although not in all countries and social security more or less guarantees our future. Today what men and women seek above all in marriage is not to be alone, to love one another and to create a home in which everything can be shared as a stable project.

Moreover science and modern technology permits birth control, which used not to be the case. Thus parenthood changes into a responsible attitude in the service of interpersonal and fruitful love.

This is indisputably a step forward, although some traditionalist groups are putting up strong resistance to it. Apart from the remnants of puritanism that may be mixed up in this attitude, perhaps it also contains a certain ecological bias—natural methods—and the subconscious fear that when sexual relations are cut off from their immediate connection with children, sexual life ceases to be a monopoly of the home which is then subjected to a sexual explosion with most serious consequences.

4. FORECASTS FOR THE FUTURE

It is very difficult to foresee how far the sexual revolution we are in the middle of now will go. However what is certain is that not everything will depend on it. There is no reason to overvalue the positive transcendant side of sexuality just because the negative was overemphasised in the past, although this latter of course was worse. But sexuality has an indisputable social resonance and the sexual revolution will affect in some way or another the social changes that accompany the passage from the industrial to the post-industrial age.

(a) Being more than doing and having

In the first place it looks as if we are moving towards a society which, unlike industrial society, lays more importance on being than on doing and having. We need to have things, indeed more than previously and with less effort, but not for the sake of a consumerist lust to possess, but in order to be and not just to be an isolated individual but be with others, us.

There is no doubt that in this sense what we have called diffuse sexuality can help to break down many barriers which have traditionally separated men and women.

(b) Democratisation of friendship

Friendship has existed from time immemorial, as we discover in Hebrew and Greek literature. But it was an aristocratic luxury for exquisite and privileged souls. Today it

E

looks as if we are seeing a process of democratisation of friendship. The re-valuing of the person as such and of his or her unquestionable rights as well as of interpersonal relations have been largely responsible for this. This exchange between me and you is especially valid in the case of the interpersonal relations between men and women.

(c) 'Siblingisation' of sexuality

The living together of the two sexes in recent years—collaboration at work, co-education, unisex—has produced, contrary to what many expected, a phenomenon of sexual cooling. It has decreased the initial effervescence and slowly there has developed what we might call a sexual brother-and-sisterliness. From falling in love like a thunderbolt, in which sexual attraction is primary, there has been a gradual change towards love and friendship, in which the most important thing is mutual admiration, a bit like what happened at the beginning of culture with the passage from the endogamous to the exogamous family and the prohibition of incest between siblings and first cousins.

(d) Opening up of the family

Finally the sexual revolution, together with other psycho-social factors such as the need to create intermediate entities between the self-enclosed individual and the vast alienated and alienating mass, is contributing to what we might call an opening up of the family as a community way of life. Thus we arrive at group marriage or a marriage of families. Not like old fashioned communes which grouped together individuals of different sex, which collapsed almost everywhere, but on the lines of a community based on your own front door and autonomous families.

At one level these families retain an absolute autonomy and independence, but on another level they have a permanent commitment to each other, which enables them to feel that they are a real family of families.

By this opening up, the urban nuclear family can compensate for the reduction in numbers and skills that it suffered when it passed from the agricultural to the urban age. It will resolve the problem of marginalisation to which children, the sick, the old and the subnormal are exposed in the urban nuclear family, as they were not in the rural patriarchal family. It will open the way to the post-industrial world by integrating community activity with the initiative of isolated individuals and multiplicatory mass dynamism.

Translated by Dinah Livingstone

John Coleman

The Homosexual Revolution and Hermeneutics

THROUGHOUT THE centuries homosexuality has represented the last sexual taboo. Even in those cultures which have tolerated some open acknowledgement or expression of homosexuality it has, generally, been highly restricted or socially contained. In the Western societies since the nineteenth century, when the modern term, homosexuality, first began to be used, religion, medicine and the law have joined forces to condemn it as sinful, pathological and a crime. Since the turn of the century in particular, the medical establishment has displaced religion as the key *social* source for defining homosexual orientation and behaviours.

One author has suggested that 'homosexuality has been so completely condemned by society that society has never attempted to regulate it. There are no traditions or conventions or rules properly belonging to it . . . Homosexuality has been without form. It presents an anarchic domain in which the participants are left to make their own rules as they go along'.[1]

A strong conspiracy of silence has reigned over the subject of 'the love that dare not speak its name'. Even in enlightened circles of sex educators, homosexuality still remains the great absent topic.[2] Until very recently any objective treatment of homosexuality was invisible in history, literature, the cinema and the public media. Later, its portrayal in, for example, the film was almost uniquely in stereotypical distorted or grotesque forms.[3] Even scholarly treatises concerning homosexuality in ancient Greece are of very recent vintage due to censorship of the facts.[4] This conspiracy of silence, including the silence of homosexuals themselves, made it almost impossible for homosexuality to have a social and public form of its own.

Only in the last decade have we even begun to recover some aspects of the history of this minority, its self-understanding and the gradual emergence of its own organisation, communities and discourse. Since the sexual revolution, important segments of the homosexual population have organised into a community of shared discourse with its own appropriate organisational networks, press and political agenda. Indeed, as I will argue, in the advanced industrial societies, one effect of the sexual revolution has been that homosexuals now constitute, for the first time in modern history, a self-conscious community with its own distinctive public interpretation of the meaning, purposes and political and social goals of homosexuality. In that sense, homosexuality is no longer totally without form, traditions, conventions or rules of proper conduct of its own. It proposes its own hermeneutic for understanding religion, homosexuality and society.

There are several distinctive sociological pre-conditions for the emergence of a homosexual revolution of consciousness. It will be important to recognise that the precise meaning of homosexuality is embedded in culturebound and historically specific locales, cultures, traditions and social groupings. For, as Michel Foucault has insisted, when dealing with the question of sexuality we can not engage in a-historical speculations.[5] Like every other human phenomenon, sexuality—its meanings, expressions, discourses and cultural channeling—is the product of history and culture and is, thus, embedded through and through with history. Hence, for example, the very term, homosexuality, is the product of a late nineteenth century medical point of view which began to speak of homosexuals as a distinctive class of people, thereby breaking with an earlier pattern of merely noting sexual behaviours, without attending to the issue of sexual orientation as a human condition. At present, most social scientists feel constrained to speak about homosexuali*ties* (in the plural) rather than of a single constellation of norms, behaviours and discourses. Very clearly, for example, lesbianism, as a social and sexual phenomenon, is quite distinct from male homosexuality.

1. SOCIOLOGICAL PRE-CONDITIONS

Most social histories of homosexual liberation point to the key factor of developed capitalist society as a pre-condition for the emergence of conscious gay identities. John D'Emilio has written a careful social history of the homosexual movement in the United States since 1940. He sums up the relationship between homosexuality and industrial capitalism:

> As a free-labor system, capitalism pulled men and women out of a household economy and into the market-place where they exchanged their industrial labor power for wages. Throughout the nineteenth and twentieth centuries, as the socialized production of commodities spread, goods formerly made in the home could be purchased. The family, deprived of the functions that once held it together as an economic unit, became instead an effective entity that nurtured children and promoted the happiness of its members. Birth rates declined steadily and procreation figured less prominently in sexual life. In place of the closely knit villages . . . huge impersonal cities arose to attract an ever larger proportion of Americans. The interlocking processes of urbanization and industrialization created a social context in which an autonomous personal life could develop. Affection, intimate relationships and sexuality moved increasingly into the realm of individual choice, seemingly disconnected from how one organized the production of goods necessary for survival. In this setting, men and women who felt a strong erotic attraction to their own sex could begin to fashion from their feeling a personal identity and a way of life.[6]

Gregory Baum has suggested, besides urbanisation and late capitalist industrial organisation, a third sociological pre-condition.

Baum argues that only in Protestant pluralist cultures could homosexuals lay public claim to an alternative life-style. He sees a paradox in the three sociological conditions for the emergence of the gay culture:

> The three conditions I have described are highly ambiguous. Protestant pluralism has produced a new individualism, undermining the possibility of organic solidarity with a people, a class or a group; urbanization initiates people into anomie and loneliness; and the late phase of capitalism creates not only a culture dedicated to consumption

but also generates giant transnational corporations with powers greater than many national governments, accountable to none, which rule the world with profit as their only goal. We touch here a dilemma of gay people. The society which has permitted them to engage in a realistic struggle for equality is precisely the society of empire and domination, the source of so much injustice in the world.[7]

2. THE TRAJECTORY OF THE LIBERATION MOVEMENT

The United States represents the nation where the homosexual revolution has made the most advances.[8] Nevertheless, the pattern exhibited by the American homosexual revolution is, by no means, unique in the industrialised world.[9] The first major homosexual organisation in the United States, The Mattachine Society, was founded in 1951. Its main purpose was educational, to raise the consciousness of American homosexuals that they constitute an oppressed minority. The Mattachine Society and the lesbian social group founded about the same time, The Daughters of Billitis, courted respectability and sought the support of establishment figures in law, psychiatry and religion.

In the late 1950s and early 1960s a series of court challenges to American censorship laws precipitated homosexuality into the public eye. A distinctively homosexual press emerged with a network of magazines and newspapers in every large American city. The emergence of the gay press cannot be overestimated as a social phenomenon. It allowed homosexuals to conceive of their condition as something other than an individual plight or destiny. The gay press inculcated the ideas of a distinctively homosexual culture and homosexuals as an oppressed minority. More importantly, for the first time in history, it created a *public* discourse by homosexuals, a self-generated hermeneutic of the meaning, possibilities and public face of homosexuality.

The gay press in the United States—with hundreds of newspapers and magazines—served as a contact point for isolated homosexuals. Moreover, it provided a fund of articles and stories about prominent homosexuals and long-term homosexual couples. It raised issues about the appropriate forms, traditions and conduct of homosexuals. What political goals should homosexuals pursue and which movements should they support? What possibilities exist for homosexuals to live a distinctively religious life? What constitutes promiscuity, responsible sexuality and appropriate commitment? Freed from earlier negative stereotypes (often internalised by homosexuals), the gay press created a uniquely homosexual moral and political discourse such that in the future no hermeneutic of the phenomenon could be credible which simply bypassed this discourse of the homosexual community itself.

In the late 1960s and the 1970s the homosexual movement in the United States became much more militant. Adopting a rhetoric and tactics similar to the black civil rights movement (and, later, the woman's movement), the American gay movement targeted four key areas: the law and politics; the media; the medical establishment; the churches. Its slogans now called for equality under the law rather than mere understanding.

3. THE LAW

The American homosexual movement has successfully challenged statutes in many states which declare private homosexual behaviour a crime. It has also been instrumental in enacting laws which punish discrimination against homosexuals in the job-market, housing and other public facilities. In many large American cities such as San Francisco, Denver, Houston and Washington, D.C., the organised homosexual vote has proved to be the swing vote which determines the outcome of elections. Hence, politicians have begun to listen to their demands. Various homosexual caucuses constitute an important factor in the Democratic Party and in the Democratic Socialists of America.

Perhaps the major political achievement of the homosexual rights groups was the inclusion in the political platform of the National Democratic Party's election programme of 1980 of a gay rights provision. Homosexuals, although a minority, represent an organised public political force to be reckoned with. Increasingly their public rights as citizens with equal privileges are recognised under the law. In many large American cities homosexual groups have been so successful in their political demands that the police force recruit openly gay persons as officers. They have also enlisted the aid of the police force in stamping out unprovoked homophobic violence against gays.

4. THE MEDIA

After the Stonewall riots in New York City in 1969 which represented a major turning point in the homosexual liberation movement, the gay liberation forces targeted the national or local news media for its refusal to circulate news stories of the gay community or for negative stereotypical coverage of gays. In many cities gays mounted their own regular radio programmes.[10]

After Stonewall, the leaders of the gay liberation forces included many who had been active in supporting the black civil rights and anti-war movements. They were politically sophisticated in the tactics of non-violent protest. Gay groups have boycotted or picketed movies and held sit-ins in television studios and magazine offices. Over the years, they have been successful in gaining more equal access to the media and in injecting a new form of discourse about homosexuality into the public eye.

In general, this homosexual message has sought to shift the focus of interpretation of homosexuality from the view of gays as 'flawed individuals' toward the notion of homosexuals as an oppressed minority in American society. The gay liberation leaders insist that homosexuality is not so much a mere individual variance as an instance of systematic injustice, a denial of human dignity and rights similar to discriminations against blacks, Hispanics and women.·

Moreover, the gay movement has been able to organise several boycotts of industrial products. Their message to industrial capitalism has been that homosexuals represent a sophisticated and affluent market for goods and services. It is claimed that the homosexual community will successfully withhold its purchasing power from products produced by companies which discriminate against gays. More and more, many American firms have consciously catered, in direct or subliminal advertising and through other means, to the nearly 20,000,000 gays in the United States.

5. THE MEDICAL MODEL

Probably the greatest single success of the homosexual movement has been its assault on the medical model of homosexuality which prevailed until the 1970s. A number of prominent social scientists and sexologists such as Alfred Kinsey, Harold Becker and Evelyn Hooker had conducted studies of the homosexual community which were sympathetic to the plight of discrimination. Hooker, especially, focused her studies on 'healthy' homosexuals. With the help of these sympathetic social scientists and psychologists gays engineered a successful challenge to the prevailing medical model of homosexuality as a pathology. In the early 1970s The American Association of Psychiatrists as well as the American Psychological Association went on record that homosexuality, *per se*, would no longer be considered as a pathological condition. Most psychologists have come to agree with Alan Bell who comments that 'homosexuality is a sexual variation well within the normal range of psychological functioning'.[11] Since the medical model of pathology had been widely invoked as the primary justification for laws allowing various legal discriminations against homosexuals, the demise of the medical model of pathology represents a potent social victory for the gay rights movement. Now recognised as deserving a range of rights under the law, homosexuals did not need to remain invisible. Once visible, they could create their own community with its own social forms.

6. RELIGION AND HOMOSEXUALITY

The relation between homosexual groups and religion has been complicated. Early in the 1960s the American homosexual leaders began to find supporters among ministers of liberal Protestant churches. The first major organisation within the churches was the San Francisco based Council on Religion and the Homosexual (CHR) in 1964. *CHR* members took advantage of the theological ferment and social activism which permeated the liberal churches in the 1960s to push for a re-examination of Christian attitudes toward same-sex eroticism. *CHR* brought ministers together from around the country for symposia on homosexuality.

CHR spawned similar councils in cities such as Dallas, Los Angeles, Washington, D.C., and Seattle. By 1966 the National Council of Churches began to hold nationally sponsored symposia on the issue.

Anthropologist Michael Gorman has written a doctoral dissertation at the University of Chicago in which he argues that the proliferation of gay religious caucuses and congregations within the main-line churches after 1969 was a response to the new situation of the gay community after the Stonewall riots. The gay community had decided to 'come out of the closet' as individuals and as a community. It began to mark out distinctive enclaves and neighbourhoods in every large American city with functions similar to ethnic urban enclaves. It also began to expand its network of organisations beyond bars and bathhouses to include gay community centres, athletic groups, serious bookstores, discussion groups, political organisations and caucuses of gay lawyers, doctors and other professional groups.

Within the space of mere months after the Stonewall riots, with their avowed aim of building a distinctively public homosexual community of belonging and discourse, almost every Protestant church began to include homosexual congregations and caucuses (e.g. *Integrity* in the Protestant Episcopal Church; *Affirmation* in the Methodist church and *Evangelicals Concerned* in more fundamentalist churches). Besides the exclusively gay Metropolitan Community Church with congregations in more than 100 American cities, there also exists a national Catholic organisation of gay congregations (*Dignity*) with over 100,000 members. There are also gay synogogues.

Gorman argues, persuasively, that these religious caucuses and congregations perform the classic Durkheimian function for religion whereby religion represents a socially cohesive and legitimating force for community. If, Gorman contends, the homosexual community in America desired to be considered a recognisable *community* it would need to mirror the religious face of ordinary religious communities. With its ecumenical consortium of Protestant-Catholic-Jew, the homosexual community came to resemble ordinary mainline communities.

It is perhaps symptomatic of the social importance of religion in American society that the first book-length portrayal of an urban homosexual community looked to the modern civil pattern of religious tolerance as a model for homosexuals to follows:

The best solution to the problem of homosexuality is one which is *modeled on the solution to the problem of religious difference*, namely, a radical tolerance for homosexual object-choice, whether as a segment of an individual's sexual existence or as a full commitment to homosexuality as a way of life.[12]

Christian gays have attempted a hermeneutic of suspicion concerning the traditional Christian condemnation of *all* same-sex expression of genital love. The general lines of this hermeneutic of suspicion include the following elements:

(*a*) A recognition of systematic distortion in communicating about homosexuality in Western culture, generally, has led many to question whether the churches have not also shared in this distortion. For example, many wonder what interpretative theory of scripture is operative when Leviticus 18:22 is cited as an authoritative condemnation of homosexuality while other taboos in Leviticus (e.g. the defilement of menstruating women) are ignored. A growing number of theologians and biblical scholars have argued that from scriptures alone neither a comprehensive blessing of same-sex committed love nor an absolute prohibition is possible.

(*b*) Other theologians and gay groups, following the hermeneutic of women's groups, have questioned whether a systematic communication distortion concerning sexuality is not involved in the inheritance, from Augustine, of deep suspicions of any expression of sexuality (in Augustine, even within marriage) and the persistent linkage and over-identification in Christian history between sexuality and sin.

(*c*) Several churches, most notably the Methodist church, have come to recognise the importance of *homophobia* (an irrational compulsive fear and disgust of homosexuality caused by the inability of persons to acknowledge homosexual feeling in themselves) in many church members. Since most of the churches in the first world draw their congregations largely from a middle-class clientele, the question is posed whether the churches have not shared in what is, fundamentally, a socially-conditioned bourgeois respectability ethic in matters of homosexuality.

The zealous denial or erasure of homosexuality from even history and scholarship represents a systematic distortion of the historical evidence necessary for a full hermeneutic of homosexuality. Few topics are so emotion-laden. John Boswell has noted the presence of systematic distortions in achieving objectivity in writing the history of homosexual consciousness. 'The history of minorities poses ferocious difficulties: censorship and distortion, absence or destruction of records, the difficulty of writing about personal and private aspects of human feelings and behavior, political dangers attendant on choosing certain subjects.'[13] Recognising the existence of homophobia, the Methodist Church has suggested that any Christian hermeneutic of the issue of homosexuality also address homophobia as a reality which distorts the record.

(*d*) Perhaps most tellingly, the churches have found it very difficult, if not impossible, to admit the possibility of forms of homosexual maturity, responsibility and holiness. They lack visible models and imagination about homosexual holiness and the ways same-sex love could be possibly conducive to human flourishing.

James and Evelyn Whitehead address this issue. They refer to lesbian and gay Christians who 'come out' publicly:

In so doing, their life and vocation become a public witness of homosexual and Christian maturing and a gift to the next generation. Such a life provides for both homosexual and heterosexual Christians an image of what it is to mature as a Catholic and gay . . . Where there was once a void ('Do *you* know any gay Catholics?') patterns of Christian homosexual maturing begin to appear. It is possible! It becomes publicly imaginable to be both homosexual and a mature Christian. Many believers have known this for some time, but it was information not publicly available, it was not part of the church's social imagination.

Closeted lives, however holy, cannot provide images and models of religious maturing. A certain public exposure and light is required for this virtue of generativity to have its effect.[14]

The Whiteheads seem to argue that part of a full religious hermeneutic for homosexuality would allow homosexual Christians to tell their *religious* stories. Certainly those who have ministered to Catholic homosexual groups such as *Dignity* in retreats, spiritual direction and social concern for the poor and dying seem compelled to use some such language such as 'Christian maturity' and 'holiness' to describe the generous lives of some homosexual Christians they have met. They insist that these lives of struggling commitment and holiness form part of a full hermeneutic of the meaning of homosexuality.

(e) A final area of suspicion concerning the Christian teaching on homosexual behaviour centres on the way in which questions of sexuality are inevitably linked to independent issues of authority—the authority of the scriptures and of magisterial teaching. Preoccupation with defending the magisterial teaching's authority or that of scripture could lead, it is claimed, to a systematic distortion which precludes an integrated moral evaluation which, besides scripture and tradition, would insist on the role of experience as an indispensable component in moral evaluation.

A hermeneutic of suspicion concerning possible systematic communication distortions in the churches' teaching on sexuality is just that: a series of suspicions. It does not preclude the possibility of an integral re-statement of the tradition after it has passed through the objections of the hermeneutic of suspicion. One result of the impact of the homosexual revolution in the churches, however, is that no hermeneutic of homosexuality is likely to be credible which does not seriously entertain and confront these suspicions as part of its normative hermeneutic of homosexuality.

Moreover, the new situation for a hermeneutic of homosexuality since the gay liberation movements consists in the product of a public discourse by homosexuals themselves—including claims to moral rights, to a life's partner and to acknowledgement of their religious experience as Christian homosexuals. Once without form or public tradition, the homosexual community in the United States is represented by literally thousands of community institutions. Gay men and lesbians have formed their own churches, health clinics, counselling services, social centres, professional associations and amateur sports leagues. Male and female entrepreneurs have established record companies, publishing houses, magazines, literary journals, film collectives and networks of discussion groups. These have given expression to a distinctive cultural experience. As John D'Emilio notes, 'The subculture of homosexuals became less exclusively erotic. Gayness and lesbianism began to encompass an identity that for many included a wide array of private and public activities.'[15]

It is also possible to mount a hermeneutic of suspicion concerning the many moral and religious claims of homosexuals. Thus, some authors have criticised the conformism, élitism and exclusive male-bonding of certain gay views. The lesbian—and, more generally, the woman's—movement have, for example, mounted a severe critique of certain homosexual male attitudes toward the woman's movement. The irony is that, since homosexuals have experienced societal oppression, they should be able to sympathise with other oppressed groups. As 'invisibly' oppressed, they should be perceptive critics of the social order. Some, however, adopt an earlier regnant model of conformism, élitism and exclusive and exclusionary male-bonding.

Other criticisms of the new gay hermeneutic focus on the facile consumerism which is promoted by much of the gay press. Noting the economic affluence and independence of most homosexuals who do not need to support families, Matthew Fox has argued, 'This kind of economic independence sets the middle-class gay person up as an easy victim to advertisers, who are missionaries of the consumer religion of our time. The insatiable greed for the latest fashion and consumer product must be resisted by the homosexual of the middle-class.'[16]

Still another criticism, strongly urged by the woman's movement, focuses on the homosexual glorification of youth and the beautiful body similar to the prevalent attitudes toward women in modern societies. It is argued that this too easily fixates erotic interest in an alienating process of impersonalisation by making the object of sexual interest a mere *object*. The woman's movement's pervasive criticism of pornography has been levelled equally against homosexual pornography (a prominent feature of advertisements in the gay press). This complaint has led some serious gay bookstores such as, for example, the Oscar Wilde bookstore in Greenwich Village, to refuse to trade in gay pornography.

A key source of critique focuses on the pre-packaged life-style typical of many urban gays, the so-called 'cloning' phenomenon. Others note the promiscuity of many urban gays. Especially since the arrival of the mystery immune-system disease, the gay community has strongly debated responsible sexuality and the search for permanent partners. Finally, many point to the ways in which homosexuals, similar in this to other persecuted groups, often internalise the societal stereotypes or fall prey to some of the worse sins of modern, capitalistic consumer societies: 'Power over, power under, sadomasochism consumerism, hatred of body, inability to sustain relationships, adolescent arrest and egoistic quests for perfectionism and immortality.'[17] These pathologies, rather than the homosexual condition as such, it is argued, need to command the best moral efforts of gays.

It is noteworthy that the homosexual press and gay discussion groups have at least entertained most of these various suspicions of the moral integrity of a gay life-style. As a community of discourse, the gay movement has become capable of self-criticism. Like every human phenomenon, the gay liberation movement contains moral and religious ambiguities. The great moral achievement of the gay liberation movement has been to help homosexuals overcome crippling and self-destructive self-rejection and alienation and to create a community with interests beyond mere erotic attraction. As a political movement it has sought an extension of political equality and freedom, fought unfair discriminations against homosexuals and joined forces with blacks, the woman's movement and other groups working for a more just and equitable society based on respect for human dignity wherever it is found.

Together with the woman's movement, the homosexual liberation movement represents, organisationally, the most stunning sociological achievement to result from the sexual revolution. Beginning in the 1960s as a tentative collective of furtive individuals, it has successfully mounted attacks on the law, the medical model of homosexuality and homophobia in the churches. It has produced, for the first time in history, a *public* discourse by homosexuals about homosexuality, with its own set of moral and religious claims. No hermeneutic of homosexuality will probably, ever again, be able to by-pass a dialogue with these claims.

For the Christian, ambiguities are bound to remain about the permissability of some forms of homosexual life-style and behaviour. Many feel the long tradition of condemnation by scripture and *magisterium* are binding. Few will expect imminent major changes in Catholic teaching. Many will argue that while no *one* source of moral tradition (scripture, natural law, traditional church teaching or human experience) can yield a comprehensive blessing or a comprehensive condemnation of all same-sex genital activity that, nevertheless, the burden of all four elements taken together will continue to affirm a heterosexual norm.

Lisa Cahill who has argued just this point, contends, nevertheless:

To the extent that homosexual love is characterized by fidelity and service, by sacrifice and liberation, by repentence and reconciliation, it follows Jesus' teaching and example. The larger community must include homosexuals also in their attitudes of forgiveness and reconciliation as well as judgement ... Far from branding all constitutional homosexuals as 'sinners' in the specific sense, Christian ethics accepts the fact of homosexuality or heterosexuality as beyond the control of most individuals. Certainly, homosexual persons (sexually active or celibate) are not inhibited by their sexuality from relying on their character to realize morally commendable qualities or qualities consistent with their faith in Jesus Christ and life within the community. The cultivation of love, self-sacrifice, fidelity and service are even more important for Christian moral agents that avoidance of the specific sorts of conduct which are *in general* not expressive of those virtues.[18]

I have argued, in this article, that the major sociological achievement of the homosexual liberation movement has been the production, for the first time in history, of a public discourse and self-generated hermeneutic of homosexuality. Homosexuality is no longer without form, traditions or rules of proper conduct. It constitutes what anthropologists would call a culture.

Whatever the many moral and religious ambiguities of the new homosexual culture and discourse, it promises liberation, dignity and self-respect for a long oppressed minority. To the extent that it attacks narrow concepts of sex-gender roles it also promises liberation to heterosexuals as well who might be freed from narrow gender stereotypes. The new homosexual discourse proposes a society respectful of human dignity and variety. Minimally, the task for the churches would seem to be to sift carefully and discern the moral and religious claims implicit in this self-generated hermeneutic of homosexuals. Because of its theological claims to correlate Christian tradition with human experience, it would seem impossible to achieve a genuinely modern Christian hermeneutic for homosexuality if dialogue (which is never the same as mere acceptance) with the moral and religious claims of homosexuals is simply by-passed.

Notes

1. Larry Nachman 'Genet: Dandy of the Lower Depths' in *Homosexuality: Sacrilege, Vision, Politics* ed. Robert Boyers and George Steiner (N.Y. 1983) p. 360.

2. See Gabriel Moran 'Education: Sexual and Religious' in *A Challenge to Love* ed. Robert Nugent (N.Y. 1983) p. 161.

3. For a comprehensive view of gay stereotypes in the film, see Vito Russo *The Celluloid Closet* (N.Y. 1981).

4. For the systematic suppression of evidence of Greek homosexuality until recent times, see Thomas Lewis 'The Brothers of Ganymede' in *Sacrilege, Vision, Politics* pp. 147–65.

5. See Michel Foucault *The History of Sexuality* I (N.Y. 1981).

6. John D'Emilio *Sexual Politics, Sexual Communities* (Chicago 1983) p. 11.

7. Gregory Baum 'The Homosexual Condition and Political Responsibility' in *A Challenge to Love* p. 46.

8. See for this history, Toby Morotta *The Politics of Homosexuality* (N.Y. 1981).

9. For a non-American example of homosexual liberation, see Jeffrey Weeks *Coming Out: Homosexual Politics in Britain* (London 1977).

10. For the gay press, see William Spiegelman 'The Progress of a Genre: Gay Journalism and its Audience' in *Homosexuality: Sacrilege, Vision, Politics* pp. 308–25.

11. In 'Homosexuality: an Overview' in *Male and Female: Christian Approaches to Sexuality* ed. Ruth Barnhouse and Urban Holmes (N.Y. 1976).

12. Martin Hoffman *The Gay World* (N.Y. 1968) pp. 197–98.

13. John Boswell 'Revolutions, Universals and Sexual Categories' in *Homosexuality: Sacrilege, Vision, Politics* p. 93.

14. James and Evelyn Whitehead 'Three Passages of Maturity' in *Challenge to Love* p. 184.

15. D'Emilio, the work cited in note 6, p. 239.

16. Matthew Fox 'The Spiritual Journal of the Homosexual' in *The Challenge to Love* p. 193.

17. *Ibid.* p. 190.

18. Lisa Cahill 'Moral Methodology: A Case Study' in *Chicago Studies* Summer (1980) p. 32.

Jacques Lazure

Young People, Sexuality, and Political Contestation

TO BEGIN with, the fields of politics and of sexuality seem pretty remote from one another. As the result of the complex process of social differentiation which advanced industrial societies have undergone, each of these fields has worked out for itself a sphere of relative autonomy where it develops according to its own dynamic nature, its own particular needs and its own specific effects. This has reached the point where in social and intellectual discussion each is accorded its own niche: one within the category of what is public, legitimate, logical and rational, and technical; the other within the more shadowy and unforeseeable category of what is private, subjective, passionate and often illicit, there where our most secret desires and dreams multiply.

1. YOUTH IN SOCIETY

Nevertheless, reality is concerned to bridge the gap between these two aspects of society. They are in fact much more in touch with each other than one might believe. But it is not easy to disentangle these close and constant relations between politics and sexuality. Still less is it so, we must add, when young people are involved. On the one hand, we all know how the development of sexuality, relationships between boys and girls (or, with the increasing phenomenon of homosexuality, between young people of the same sex), the diversity of sexual experiences or adventures represent a central preoccupation of young people, let us say between the ages of fifteen and twenty-five. This is all the more so in the present situation of young people. For at least the past twelve years or so this has been marked by the withering, if not the complete disappearance, of the claims they were making and the great movements that supported these claims, by their becoming turned in on themselves (whether as individuals struggling to survive or as members of small communities of equals set up on a human scale and with human warmth), and by their pronounced interest in everything affecting their personal autonomy, freedom, and development.

On the other hand, it is important to realise the extent to which, at least in the advanced industrial countries of the Western hemisphere (including Japan), young people today are not interested in politics. In general, the attitude they display towards it is one of indifference, of disillusionment, indeed of cynicism. Plenty of studies and surveys have shown that young people take no notice of politics and of party struggles, whose technological and bureaucratic entanglements they are often unable to unravel. And if by chance they succeed in grasping the profound human and social values at stake, it is to deplore the fact that politics too easily conjures these away and takes little account of the values and needs of which they are at present aware. The radical struggles conducted recently by young people, above all by students, came up against thick barriers of incomprehension and of social resistance, when they did not receive the counter-blows of political repression. Social and political contestation by young people has given way to their disengagement and their demobilisation.

2. RETREAT FROM POLITICS

The growing distance between their lack of interest in politics and their preoccupation with more personal and communal values of development, at the heart of which is to be found the emancipation of their sexuality and its growth towards maturity, contributes towards strengthening the institutional language, tinged with Manichaeism, which tends to oppose the public and the private and to separate them. This very fact raises still more bluntly the question of the relations between politics and sexuality among young people and the meaning that may emerge from these. Do young people's sexual values, attitudes and behaviour include some dimension of political and social contestation, or are they completely lacking in this? To put it the other way round, is the absence of political commitment among young people tantamount to their adherence or their return to conservatism and to traditional morality even with regard to their sexuality? Finally, and more generally, do young people today represent a privileged context where new and original relations are being formed between politics and sexuality? These are the questions which this article will try to answer, more particularly with regard to the young people of North America with whom we are more familiar.

The period of student conflict in the 1960s brought out particularly strongly the link among young people between a more liberal and permissive sexuality which cut social taboos to ribbons, and attitudes and behaviour which in general called into question and opposed the established social order. American sociologists like Charles Reich[1] and Theodore Roszack,[2] whose analyses of the new youth culture attracted a great deal of attention at the time, have well brought out the innovatory and transformatory character of young people's sexuality. This formed an integral part of their contestation of the various social forms of exploitation and domination. Two of the best analysts of American young people, Richard Flacks[3] and Kenneth Keniston,[4] have also shown how the young 'activists' of the 1960s came as a matter of fact from upper middle class families (European sociology would place them among the petite bourgeoisie) characterised by greater egalitarian and reforming tendencies in all fields, including sexuality. On this subject Marxist analysis of young people, which in any case is rather scanty, has not shown itself very accurate: it is not young people from the working class or the proletariat who initiated and led the struggle for sexual or other liberation. Nor today are they the protagonists in a complex of new relations being formed between sexuality and a certain global vision of society.

The close association between sexual freedom and the politics of contestation that was given shape in young people's lives in the course of the 1960s gave a certain degree of confirmation and embodiment to the ideas of Wilhelm Reich[5] and the questions he raised. His central argument was that every authoritarian society only arises and survives thanks to the ideology of conservatism that it inculcates in its members. In the masses this ideology fashions a collective mental structure composed of the absence of a critical and creative spirit, uncritical admiration for authority, dependence, indeed servility. Now this kind of mental structure arises from the guilt-inducing restraint and suppression of sexuality among young people, through the intermediary of reactionary social morality and the institution of bourgeois monogamous marriage. In this way 'the family assumes for the conservative that privileged meaning of the bulwark of the social order he believes in'.[6] If therefore you liberate young people's sexuality and arrange things so that their fundamental sexual needs are satisfied, you will obtain generations of autonomous, creative, revolutionary people, capable of throwing off the yoke of every kind of fascism and of establishing a new society for the benefit of the exploited, under the sign of freedom and responsibility.

The experience of the social and political struggles in which the student movements were engaged in the 1960s, in the context of a vision of cultural revolution in which a large part was played by the transformation of sexuality, shows in actual fact that Reich was not completely wrong in linking sexuality and politics and in wanting to remove the former's inhibitions in order to allow involvement in the latter. But what is the present state of relations between sexuality and politics at a time when the student movements no longer exist and when young people, somewhat curled in on themselves, no longer feel so much interest and devote little energy to political contestation?

The question is all the more relevant in that several analyses, notably those of Marcuse, Schelsky and Reiche, have insisted on the fundamentally integrating, reductionist and, on the whole, alienating character of the sexual liberalisation of advanced industrial societies of the capitalist kind. On this view the evolution of sexual mores in these countries would only represent finally a phenomenon of 'repressive desublimation'.[6] Again, there has been an incredible process of making sexuality uniform and standardising it, tending to 'reify' it, to reduce it to a piece of merchandise, to give it the function of an object of consumption, in a process of sexual manipulation which on this interpretation is only one of many embodiments of contemporary economic exploitation.[7] Schelsky is full of the same kind of insights: contemporary men and women become sexual beings above all through external factors, under the influence of erotic images and stereotypes transmitted by the mass media.[8] In short, according to this interpretation sexuality simply becomes absorbed with the economic and political system of capitalism.

Here we have an analysis of contemporary sexuality, particularly of young people, which moreover strikes us as simplistic and one-dimensional. It tends to pass over in silence the flagrant contradictions which are to be found at the heart of the new sexuality of young people and which pull it in all directions. For our part, we take the opposite view and hold that the general state of sexuality is neither black nor white: it is developing rather in grey areas where one finds at one and the same time both new specific forms of alienation and tenacious elements of traditional conservatism, but also where there appear new and original orientations and phenomena marked by the characteristics of contestation and liberation.

Certainly, the way sex (particularly the female variety) has been taken over by commerce and publicity in all their forms constitutes in our eyes a structural phenomenon of the flattening and imprisoning of sexuality and of its immense vital forces. Massive exposure to sex in its economic and social applications is bound to generate a conformist craze which often reinforces traditional attitudes and behaviour. Think, for example, of the macho images diffused by film, television and radio; of the double standard that is still maintained for the male's benefit; of the uninterchangeability of masculine and feminine roles which is always justified as 'natural' and unavoidable; of the very idea of the bourgeois family and marriage which is still often put forward as the only 'true' ideal of life, with its paternal authority, its reassuring economic power, its fidelity thought of too restrictively in purely genital terms, without taking any notice of the increasing number of one-parent families.

Young people do not remain insensitive to all this commercialisation of sexuality and the uniformity it creates. Many of them let themselves be bitten by the bug of conformity and involve themselves uncritically in the immediate and pleasure-seeking pursuit of the objectives of the good life as defined by society. We could even affirm that this search for instantaneous pleasure, whether sexual or other, that is so typical of the teenage culture, particularly in North America, is no small contribution to their disengagement from every form of political or social involvement. From this point of view the advanced industrial societies have truly sanitised young people and turned them into a uniform lump. We were able to establish this clearly in a recent study, as yet unpublished, of young people in the Plateau Mont-Royal, a working-class district of Montréal.

3. CRITICS OF DOMINANT CULTURE

It is no less true that the new-found sexual permissiveness of young people does not in our opinion represent a simple mechanical response to the dictates of a society geared to the consumption of goods of every kind, including sexuality. Nor does it represent a simple capitulation or complacent submission to the established order, which is to be taken as it is without any desire to change it. On the contrary, many aspects of young people's values, attitudes and sexual activities objectively entail a rejection of present society and of its predominant values, a contestation of its general orientations, and a radical questioning of the stand it takes with regard to relations between men and women, to the couple and the family, and thus to what, at least in many official statements, is regarded as the foundation stone of the whole of society. Nor is young people's sexuality deprived—far from it—of all political significance and all social impact. Even in the absence of external political or social involvement it is from many points of view opposed to society and disputes its foundations.

Certain examples of this are seen in the growing rejection of marriage or at least the lateness with which young people commit themselves to it. This is a new and very revealing phenomenon in North America. It merely indicates young people's unease, not to say confusion in the face of the perplexities of the future or the complexities of life in the present. Often it also includes a rejection that is more or less conscious but none the less real of the institutions of society in which young people no longer have confidence and of which they have been the victims.

Pointing in the same direction are their desire to live together outside marriage, at least for a time, and their actual experimentation with this kind of free relationship. We think we have shown in our study of young unmarried couples[9] how young Québécois who were living together formed part, as far as the vast majority of them were concerned, of a world of social and cultural contestation. It is true that to the extent to which this phenomenon becomes general in society it will be liable to lose its contestatory bite and see itself assimilated to the official rules of the civil law, and thus to gather to its bosom young people who will merely reproduce the more or less traditional patterns of the institution of matrimony. Nevertheless, the relationship of living together outside marriage includes in its very structure a dynamism of its own which points in a direction opposed to that of marriage. In contrast to the latter, it does not as such depend directly on any social model which has been institutionalised and which has elements of compulsion: rather, it depends on the free initiative and the creativity of the two parties who continually decide how it should be made up and what its fate should be. From this point of view it is an important factor in the long process of profound transformation of the couple and of the family.

The keener awareness among young people, and of course particularly among young women, of women's inferior status in society and their more pronounced interest in the cause of women's liberation also include a social and political dimension which makes young people both more alert to the injustices of society and more rebellious with regard to them and which inclines them more easily in due course to come into conflict with them, at least on their own account and in their own personal lives. The same applies with regard to sexual minorities, particularly homosexuals. In general, young people show the latter more tolerance and respect than adults do and are more aware of the impediments that society imposes and of the repression it exerts against such minorities.

For the rest, it strikes us as very significant that it is particularly in these fields (together with those of ecology and of a better quality of life and personal autonomy) that the young people of today are collectively engaged in actual conflicts. True, it is a very small minority of young people that is politically and socially involved, but they are to a much greater degree within movements fighting for women's liberation, sexual freedom and the quality of life in general than in political parties or movements, trade unions and student organisations in the strict sense of the term.

Basically, many more people's sex-lives are immersed in a complex of values which are more characteristically theirs. Their sexuality is expressed in terms of a youth culture of which the predominant characteristic is the quality of what is imaginary, of what is non-rational, in opposition to the logical and rational model which inspires the economic, social and political structures of adult society. Our view in fact is that society as shaped and run by adults is the chief transmitter of a culture distinguished by positivist science, by technocratic organisation and by what are termed rational norms. For many young people on the other hand, their world is rather that of the imagined, of dream, fantasy, feeling, of what is non-rational, not to say irrational.

This young people's world of the imagination finds expression in three ways in particular. With Bennett Berger,[10] we think that the youth culture shows a search for pleasure and the placing of value on it, in contrast to an adult society which sanctifies the principle of reality and efficiency. The importance young people give to the pleasure principle gives their activities an 'expressive' orientation, in contrast to the 'instrumental' orientation of adult activities. Finally, young people give a preferential position to egalitarian interpersonal relations, particularly in leisure activities and with regard to sex, in place of the authoritarian, objective and anonymous relations of bureaucracy.

It is in this cultural subsoil that young people's sexuality finds its real significance, that of objective opposition to the deeper orientations and precise directions of adult society. It is at this point where young people's sexuality finds their own cultural anchorage that the dimension arises of at least potential political and social contestation. It is not necessary that young people should be aware of it for such a dimension to exist. It is even less necessary for it to express itself in the classical revolutionary forms, whether Marxist or other, of the nineteenth and twentieth centuries.

In fact, contestation on the part of young people has shifted considerably of recent years. It has flowed back from the exterior to the interior: it has moved from traditional political conflict and from conquering the apparatus of the State to claiming one's own identity, the possibility of developing in an autonomous fashion one's creative powers, one's affections, one's physical attributes and one's personal relations. All these new preoccupations have led to a dimming of normal contestation and its becoming merely latent. But this does not imply—far from it—that young people's revolutionary potential has disappeared completely. For several years it has been smouldering beneath the embers. It seems to us that it wants to come alive again fairly rapidly, in the typically American form of the movements that are becoming more and more considerable of the 'new age',[11] of 'alternative life-styles', of the 'conspiracy of Aquarius',[12] in which creative sexuality plays an important part and in which young people are participating in increasing numbers.

What is certain is that, as Alberto Melucci says, new social movements are now emerging to fight for a redistribution of time, of space, of the body, of desire, of relationships, in individuals' daily existence.[13] This will prepare the way for a new

F

reconciliation of the public and the private, which up till now have been artificially separated. This is because 'sexuality and the body, leisure, consumption, one's relationship with nature are no longer the loci of private reward but the areas of collective resistance, of claiming expression and enjoyment against the instrumental rationality of systems'.[14]

Young people will form part of this, with among other things their emerging sexuality: indeed, it is even likely that they will represent a privileged locus of this new contestation and of the new social relationships which it will bring in its wake.

Translated by Robert Nowell

Notes

1. Charles Reich *The Greening of America* (Toronto 1971).
2. Theodore Roszack *The Making of a Counter Culture* (Garden City, NY 1969).
3. Richard Flacks 'Social and Cultural Meanings of Student Revolt: Some Informal Comparative Observations' in *Youth and Sociology* ed. Peter K. Manning and Marcello Truzzi (New Jersey 1972) pp. 325–343.
4. Kenneth Keniston *Young Radicals* (New York 1969).
5. Wilhelm Reich *The Sexual Revolution* (London 1951).
6. Herbert Marcuse *Eros and Civilization* (New York 1955); *One Dimensional Man* (London 1964).
7. Reimut Reiche *Sexualité et lutte de classes* (Paris 1974).
8. Helmut Schelsky *Sociologie de la sexualité* (Paris 1966).
9. Jacques Lazure *Le Jeune couple non marié* (Montréal 1975).
10. Bennett Berger 'On the Youthfulness of Youth Cultures' in *Youth and Sociology*, cited in note 3, pp. 52–68.
11. Mark Satin *New Age Politics. Healing Self and Society. The Emerging New Alternative to Marxism and Liberalism* (West Vancouver 1978).
12. Marilyn Ferguson *Aquarian Conspiracy: Personal and Social Transformation in the 1980s* (London 1981).
13. Alberto Melucci 'Société en changement et nouveaux mouvements sociaux' in *Sociologie et sociétés*, 10 no. 2 (October 1978) 37–52.
14. *Ibid.* 48.

PART III

Christian Reactions

Richard Grecco

Recent Ecclesiastical Teaching

1. POPE JOHN PAUL II'S THEOLOGY OF THE BODY

POPE JOHN PAUL II has used more than one hundred General Audiences to present a theology of the body'.[1] He develops his theological anthropology in three phases.[2]

(a) The pre-historical: 'From the beginning': Matt. 19:3–9

Twenty-two addresses from 5 September 1979 to 2 April 1980 outline John Paul II's meditation on Matthew 19:3–9. Jesus refers all those who would argue the indissolubility of marriage to return to 'the beginning'. John Paul II tries to follow Jesus' advice. He attempts to rediscover the original meaning of man as female and male. Establishing a theological anthropology which incorporates sexual polarity is the key, says John Paul II, to understanding indissolubility.

For John Paul II re-constructing the primordial meaning of sexuality is a universal, intuitive pursuit: first, because the redemption of the body 'guarantees continuity and unity between the hereditary state of man's sin and his original innocence' (26 Sept. '79); second, because,

> our human experience is, in this case, to some extent a legitimate means for theological interpretation, and is, in a certain sense, an indispensable point of reference which we must keep in mind in the interpretation of the 'beginning' (26 Sept. '79).

Revelation, an intuitive pursuit of the meaning of sexuality, and human experience characterise the method of the John Paul II's theology of the body.

John Paul II interprets Genesis 1 as an objective description of sexuality. Its context is 'free from any trace whatsoever of subjectivism' (12 Sept. '79). However, the second account of creation, contends John Paul II, reflects the subjective definition of man as male and female. Nineteen addresses based on the Yahwist tradition paint John Paul II's unique picture of primeval subjectivity. It is the subjective meaning of original solitude, communion, nakedness, innocence and shame which significantly distances this teaching from a rigid act oriented approach to sexual morality. The nuptial meaning of the body for today, concludes John Paul II, depends partly on how well the person consciously appropriates the return to this pristine experience of the body. In his view, it is impossible to understand our present historical state (i.e. sinfulness) without referring first to our fundamental state of innocence, our image of God as female and male (26 Sept. '79). John Paul II's analysis of 'the beginning' starts with the phenomenon of solitude. Solitude is the original act of self-consciousness. How is Adam made aware of being alone? Through a test before self and God, Adam examines the visible world of bodies and identifies them by name (Gen. 2:19). Through his dissimilarity he recognises the self as apart, as namer, alone. Naming the creatures emphasises subjectivity. Bodily visibility conveys the experience of dissimilarity but solitude is the meaning which the experience constitutes for the subject.

Recognising solitude in the world is 'self-knowledge'. But what in the world is one's self? Consciousness of solitude inaugurates the search for identity.

> For created man finds himself right from the first moment of his existence *before God as if in search* of his own entity; it could be said: in search of a definition of himself. A contemporary would say: in search of his own identity (10 Oct. '79).

For John Paul II human sexuality is set within the context of the person's search for identity.

It is significant, argues John Paul II, that the search for identity occurs in the world. It implies that consciousness and corporality grow through mutual interaction.

> Self-knowledge develops at the same rate as knowledge of the world, of all the visible creatures, of all living beings to which man has given a name to affirm his own dissimilarity with regard to them. In this way, therefore, consciousness reveals man as the one who possesses the cognitive faculty as regards *the visible world*. With this knowledge which, in a certain way, brings him out of his own being, *man* at the same time *reveals himself to himself in all the peculiarity of his being*. He is not only essentially and subjectively alone. Solitude, in fact, signifies man's subjectivity, which is constituted through self-knowledge (10 Oct. '79).

Another constituent of subjectivity is the meaning of the body itself.

> Man is subject not only because of his self awareness . . . but also on the basis of his own body. The structure of the body is such as to permit him to be the author of a truly human activity. In this activity the body expresses the person (31 Oct. '79); (see also 24 Oct. '79).

Who one is, is expressed through the body. The person does not simply *have* a body. The body is constitutive of the subject and expresses interiority. Both the structure of consciousness and self-determination, says John Paul II, is constituted through the body. This is a fact 'which cannot but be discovered when analyzing solitude' (31 Oct. '79). Although the search for identity beings in solitude, still there awaits 'the new consciousness of the sense of one's body: A sense which, it can be said, consists in a *mutual enrichment*' (14 Nov. '79). It was not good for Adam to be alone, records the Yahwist. Alone he could discover much, yet . . .

> Man becomes the image of God not so much in the moment of solitude as in the moment of communion . . . We can deduce that man became the 'image and likeness' of God not only through his own humanity, but also through the community of persons which man and woman form right from the beginning (14 Nov. '79).

Sexuality therefore, is not an attribute of the person but a constituent of subjectivity (21 Nov. '79).

From a consciousness of solitude to an awareness of communion through the sense of nakedness, innocence and shame John Paul II develops his understanding of the constituent elements of subjectivity. He concludes that 'from the beginning' the meaning of the body was nuptial: a freedom to discover totally the giftedness of the body, sexuality, and consciousness so that the person gives freely and totally of self in a mutual acceptance of the other as subject (16 Jan. '80).

On account of subjectivity the search for self-identity must include a conscious effort to realise the meaning of one's sexuality. That meaning is known through intimacy, interiority and communication:

> They see and know each other, in fact, with all the peace of the interior gaze, which creates precisely the fullness of the intimacy of persons . . . they 'communicate' on the basis of that communion of persons in which, through femininity and masculinity, they become gift for each other. In this way they reach in reciprocity a special understanding of the meaning of their own body. Now the original meaning of nakedness corresponds to that simplicity and fullness of vision, in which understanding of the meaning of the body comes about, as it were, at the very heart of their community—communion. We call it nuptial (2 Jan. '80).

This search must begin with a return to primordial experience for 'only by returning to the beginning can man resist seeing man as object and realise himself as subject' (2 Apr. '80).

(b) The historical phase: 'In the heart' Matt. 5:27–28

Jesus' reference to the lustful look as adultery 'in the heart' is the second key to understanding the experience of sexuality. Objective acts are not as important as who the person is becoming. 'Moral value is connected with the dynamic process of man's intimacy' (16 Apr. '80). From 16 April 1980 until 6 May 1981, Matthew 5:27–28 is central to the development of phase two of his anthropology: the search for self-identity which necessarily includes the primordial experience of the body as female and male must give priority to the process of interiority. When Christ qualified a lustful look as adultery 'in the heart', he appeals to the interior man (16 Apr. '80).

To unpack the historical meaning of man, John Paul II explains fear, shame, lust, disquiet, sin, struggle, adultery, eros and ethos. These do not reside in the heart. They ferment there. They shape the subject to be this or that kind of person. However, the historical experience of man is not as hopeless as these terms imply. John Paul II's anthropology and views on sexuality are neither Manichean nor pessimistic. The human heart is not totally corrupt. The power of redemption completes the work of creation (29 Oct. '80). The interior dynamic of man as female and male is being transformed by the spirit.

The following examples of the interiority of historical man highlight John Paul II's approach.

Adam's response, 'I was afraid because I was naked and I hid myself' says John Paul II, represents a new state of consciousness. Previously they had sense knowledge of nudity yet suddenly they are conscious of fear and shame.

> It is not a question here of passing from 'not knowing to knowing' but a radical change of the meaning of the original nakedness of the woman before the man and of the man before the woman (12 Dec. '79).

Physically Adam tries to cover a reality that is much deeper, personhood. The fear is of the loss of the personal. This subjective loss of meaning is a cosmic shame as well. 'It contains such a cognitive acuteness as to create a fundamental disquiet in the whole of human existence' (28 May '80).

Historically, man (as female and male) is alienated from self. This affects the *communio personarum*.

> The shame which according to the biblical narrative induces man and woman to hide from each other and their bodies, and particular their sexual differentiation confirms that the original capacity of communicating themselves to each other . . . has been shattered (4 June '80).

The alienation of the body from personhood implies a reduction of the meaning of the body to the objective. Subjective meaning is reduced. This, argues John Paul II, is what lust, in all three of its forms, is all about (30 Apr. '80). By limiting the body to object, freedom is limited. This constraint prevents the personal gift of subject: 'The relationship of the gift is changed into the relationship of appropriation' (23 July '80). Lust limits the nuptial meaning of the body (25 June '80).

The legalistic approach to adultery tends to objectify sexuality (20 Aug. '80). The objective meaning of adultery refers to a legal violation. The prophetic approach to adultery concerns subjective meaning. Adultery is a violation of the person (27 Aug. '80). It is a breakdown of a personal covenant which signifies the communion of two people. Besides fear, shame, lust, adultery, disquiet and sin 'in the heart' there is also purity. John Paul II identifies 'purity' with Paul's life in the spirit (14 and 28 Jan. '81). Purity of heart is striving to align the heart with the ethos of redemption, to confirm integral subjectivity (3 Dec. '80). John Paul II notes that the facts, situations, and institutions of Jewish society at that time provided an ethos of 'hardened hearts'. Matt. 5:27–28. According to P. Ricoeur, says John Paul II, Nietzsche, Freud and Marx were masters of suspicion of the human heart. Their philosophical, psychological, and social theories all converged on the corruption of the human heart as the fundamental principle for interpreting man. John Paul II takes extra care to insist that the Christian cannot do this. The reason is in Matthew 5:27–28. Jesus makes an appeal precisely to the heart to rise above the evil in the heart. The basis for an appeal to the heart and the foundation of hope is 'the ethos of redemption'.

> Man cannot stop at putting the heart in a state of continual and irreversible suspicion due to the manifestations of lust of the flesh and libido . . . Redemption is a truth, a reality in the name of which man must feel called, and called with efficacy . . .

> Man must feel called to rediscover, nay more, to realize the Nuptial meaning of the body and to express in this way the interior freedom of the gift . . . (29 Oct. '80).

Interiority is the subjective dynamic by which the experience of frailty and sin come to be accepted (i.e. as components of subjectivity) in order to be transformed; only then does bodily expression signify moral uprightness, self-fulfillment and spiritualisation. Only as subjective *gift* does the body convey and constitute the meaning of 'the beginning'.

(c) The eschatological phase: Matt. 22:23–33

John Paul II finds the final key to a holistic vision of man as female and male in Jesus' blunt reply to the Sadducees about marriage after death; 'You don't know the scriptures or the power of God; they will be like angels . . . men and women will not marry.'

The Resurrection, states John Paul II, completes the revelation of the body. Life in the 'other world' has an impact on the meaning of who I am and who we are as subjects. Since the Resurrection affects the person, whether celibate or married, consideration must be given to the redemption of the body. From 16 November 1981 to 10 February 1982 Matt. 22:23–33 and 1 Cor. 15 is the focus of John Paul II's attention. The Resurrection reveals the completion of subjectivity and intersubjectivity.

This concentration (of knowledge; vision) will be above all man's rediscovery of himself, not only in the depth of his own person, but also in that union which is proper to the world of persons in their psychosomatic constitution. This is certainly a union of communion.

We must think of the reality of the 'other world' in the categories of the rediscovery of a new perfect subjectivity of everyone and at the same time of the rediscovery of a new perfect intersubjectivity of all (16 Dec. '81).

This perfection of subjectivity includes the body.

The resurrection will consist in the perfect participation of all that is physical in man in what is spiritual in him . . . it will consist in the perfect realisation of what is personal in man (9 Dec. '81). The resurrection constitutes the definitive accomplishment of the redemption of the body (27 Jan. '81).

Because of the meaning of pre-historical and historical man John Paul II is anxious to deny that the spiritualisation or divinisation of the body has anything to do with disincarnation or dehumanisation (2 Dec. '81 and 9 Dec. '81). Christ's words, says John Paul II, 'seem to affirm . . . that human bodies, recovered and at the same time renewed in the Resurrection, will keep their masculine or feminine peculiarity' (2 Dec. '81 and 13 Jan. '82). The person retains her or his psychosomatic nature. Yet, John Paul II is equally anxious to point out that the resurrection 'signifies a realisation of the primacy of the Spirit' (9 Dec. '81). The person exists in a new way. The body is both dominated and permeated by the Spirit (9 Dec. '81). He says the person is divinised or spiritualised. 'The Resurrection means a new submission of the body to the spirit' (2 Dec. '81).

The Resurrection is an experience available to historical man on account of 'the beginning' and on account of Christ. Relying on Pauline texts, John Paul II connects the phases of anthropology. 'Every man bears in himself the Image of Adam and every man also is called to bear in himself the image of Christ, the Image of the Risen One' (3 Feb. '82). The reality of the Resurrection is connected therefore to the experience of historical man in an existential way. 'It is a reality ingrafted in the man of "this world", a reality that is developed in him toward final completion' (3 Feb. '82). Each person experiences eschatological reality. Each person is in touch with 'eschatological man' (9 Dec. '81), because the human body bears in itself

the 'potentiality for Resurrection', that is, the aspiration and capacity to become definitively 'incorruptible, glorious, full of dynamism, spiritual', this happens because, persisting from the beginning in psychosomatic unity of the personal being, he can receive and reproduce in this 'earthly' image and likeness of God also the 'heavenly' image of the second Adam, Christ (3 Feb. '82). (See also 13 Jan. '82).

About revelation, John Paul II is explicit. It not only conveys conceptual information, but on account of the body enables 'the historical body to go beyond the sphere of its experience of the body' (16 Dec. '81). Christ reveals truth but the truth of a humanly experienced reality. Furthermore, adds John Paul II, the truth about both dimensions is unavailable to empirical and rationalistic methods (13 Jan. '82).

John Paul II then proceeds to discuss celibacy and virginity. He bases thirteen addresses from 10 March 1982 to 21 July 1982 on Matt. 19:11–12 and 1 Cor. 7. Then from 28 July 1982 to 15 December 1982 sixteen audiences delve into the sacrament of marriage. He bases these meditations on Ephesians 5:21–33. Both marriage and celibacy must be understood in the context of a Christian anthropology which takes a holistic view of pre-historical, historical and eschatological experience.

John Paul II concludes with three very interesting presentations on the language of the body. The person embodies the language of the Spirit.

> He has already been constituted in such a way from the 'beginning', in such wise that the most profound words of the Spirit—words of love, of giving, of fidelity—demand an adequate 'language of the body'. And without that they cannot be fully expressed (12 Jan. '83).

Relying on the Prophets and Paul, John Paul II identifies the body as the primordial sacrament of creation, of the person and of God. Its feminine and masculine structure expresses the complexity of meaning which is called Covenant. Conjugal behaviour involves a language of tenderness expressing love, fidelity, uprightness and union. This language corresponds to the meaning authored by God in the very constitution of man 'from the beginning' (26 Jan. '83).

> If the prophetic texts indicate conjugal fidelity and chastity as 'truth' and adultery or harlotry, on the other hand, as 'non-truth' as a falsity of the 'language of the body', (then) this happens because . . . the subject (that is, Israel as a Spouse) is in accord with the spousal significance which corresponds to the human body (because of its masculinity or femininity) in the integral structure of the person (12 Jan. '83).

For John Paul II it is not so much a question of authoring one's own body language. It is a language 'which God originated, by creating man as male and female, which Christ renewed' (19 Jan. '83). The issue is to rediscover and re-read the language which once bespoke the subject. Re-reading this language in truth is an 'indispensable' condition of the sacrament (19 Jan. '83).

2. REMARKS

One reviewer ardently characterises John Paul II's theology of sexuality as 'revolutionary'.[3] Probably this is an exaggeration. Nevertheless, John Paul II's originality does compel a degree of enthusiasm.

First, John Paul II is offering theological understanding, not simply rules about sexual behaviour. There is here the potential to modify the ethical model of official Church teaching. Whereas a legalistic model for sexual ethics emphasised the objective meaning of sexuality,[4] John Paul II's theology of the body attends to the subjective dimension. This anthropological development is the most salient feature in recent ecclesiastical teaching. It promotes a personalistic model for ethical theory.

Second, instead of a natural law theory expressed in a Neo-scholastic language, John Paul II's method is experiential. An extensive reliance on biblical texts, a conviction about the intuitive pursuit of the meaning of sexuality and the attempt to connect these to human experience typify John Paul II's methodology.

Third, his new emphasis on subjectivity and experience steers a course away from rationalism towards a wider and more relational appreciation of the ways of knowing. Intimacy, tenderness, spontaneity, body language and interiority are non-rationalistic modes of learning and growing.

Originality can tease the imagination, inspire the mind, challenge the spirit and move the heart, yet leave the person free. It is one indicator that motivation not indoctrination is the objective of the educator. Because originality tends to motivate there is a pedagogical reason for enthusiasm. Because this quality is especially important in matters moral, there is pastoral cause for further study of John Paul II's work.

Finally, there are a few questions that need exploration.

(a) About Subjectivity. John Paul II pays relative inattention to the social sciences and this has consequences. For example, of man and woman he says, 'their conjugal union presupposes a mature consciousness of the body' (21 Nov. '79). The way to such 'maturity' entails a search in all three dimensions of experience. But developmental theories of consciousness indicate that many, if not most people never achieve the high degree of authentic subjectivity that he describes.[5] Can Church teaching realistically presuppose such keenly developed levels of subjectivity? If empirical data show that it cannot, then is not the implication a revision to the Church's teaching on indissolubility?

(b) About terminology. What do the terms 'experience', 'eschatological man' and 'ethos' mean? Sometimes 'experience' refers to sense-knowledge, at other times to aspects of self-consciousness or intuition. 'Eschatological man', despite John Paul II's three phase approach, seems to refer exclusively to a thoroughly unrealised eschaton. 'Ethos' at times refers to the state of redemption and at other times to cultural norms opposed to the Gospel. These terms are a few examples which indicate an ambiguity[6] in John Paul II's approach.

(c) About the structure of consciousness. John Paul II's approach to the meaning of the body seems to be overly structured, almost mechanistic or pre-programmed. His emphasis, for example, on re-creating, re-constructing, re-discovering the meaning and then re-reading the language of the body appears somewhat exaggerated. What does such an emphasis say about the spontaneity of human expression and about human creativity and individuality?

The ecclesiastical teaching identified in this report as Pope John Paul II's theology of the body is original on account of its emphasis on subjectivity, its methodology, and its avoidance of rationalism. This uniqueness raises many interesting questions. Both the originality and the questions it poses may indicate a shift in ecclesiastical teaching. Undoubtedly, they are cause for further study.

Notes

1. All references are to the date of the audience itself. The quotations are taken from the English edition of the *Osservatore Romano*.

2. The 'total vision of Man' must integrate all three dimensions of anthropology, past, present, future. (2 Apr. '80).

3. Marcel Clément 'Une Théologie de la Sexualité' in *L'Homme Nouveau*, no. 797 (1 Nov. '81) p. 1, published in France, Belgium and Canada. This is his first in a series of fifteen commentaries: 798 (15 Nov. '81), 799 (6 Dec. '81), 800 (20 Dec. '81), 801 (3 Jan. '82), 802 (17 Jan. '82), 803 (7 Feb. '82), 804 (21 Feb. '82), 805 (7 Mar. '82), 806 (21 Mar. '82), 807 (4 Apr. '82), 808 (18 Apr '82), 809 (2 May '82) 810 (16 May '82). It is preceded by 'Les fondements de la théologie de Jean-Paul' par Aline Lizotte, 796 (18 Oct. '81).

4. The 'Declaration on Certain Questions Concerning Sexual Ethics' is a good example of such an approach. For a precise summary of theological opinion on this see Richard A. McCormick SJ *Notes on Moral Theology 1965 through 1980* (Washington 1981) pp. 668–682.

5. For example, the six stages of moral development theorised by Lawrence Kohlberg; see

'Education for Justice: A Modern Statement of the Platonic View' in *Moral Education: Five Lectures* (Cambridge Mass: Harvard Press 1970) 57–83. For a theological attempt to connect the developmental theories of Piaget, Erikson, and Kohlberg with a transcendental theory of conscience see Walter E. Conn, *Conscience: Development and Self-Transcendence* (Birmingham, Alabama 1981). James W. Fowler has utilised a developmental approach to explain the process of faith. 'Faith Development Theory and the Aims of Religious Socialization' in *Emerging Issues in Religious Education* ed. Gloria Durka and Joanmarie Smith (New York 1976) pp. 187–208, and his *Life Maps: Conversations on the Journey of Faith* (Waco, Texas 1978), see also his 'Stages in Faith, The Structural-Developmental Approach' in *Values and Moral Development* ed. Thomas C. Hennessy SJ (New York 1976) pp. 173–223.

6. Ronald Modras explores the ambiguity of John Paul II's personalistic ethics in 'The Moral Philosophy of Pope John Paul II in *Theological Studies* 41 (Dec. 1980) 683–697.

Xavier Thévenot

New Developments in Sexual Morality

AS THE preceding articles have emphasised, for several decades we have been witnessing a sexual revolution and a flowering of anthropological research into sexuality which seem to undermine the norms developed by the Christian tradition. In what ways is moral theology today trying to deal with this situation? This article is an attempt to give a brief answer to that question. It will be less an examination of the international theological literature, with which the author is insufficiently familiar, than an indication of the directions which moralists seem to be taking in their effort to produce an ethical discourse which our contemporaries will find relevant.

First, though, let me give a general impression. I have the feeling that, after a period of disarray which showed itself in reactions of fear and feelings of inferiority or guilt, leading to reticence or an uncomfortable retreat to the positions of the past, moralists specialising in questions of sexual ethics now have the confidence to speak up without complexes. This is reflected in two main attitudes, which are complementary, and indeed are classical reactions to anything new. There is an attempt to integrate what seems valid in the present 'sexual revolution', and a prophetic desire to challenge society arising out of familiarity with the word of God which always reveals itself as madness in the terms of the world's would-be wisdom.

This twofold attitude has become possible because present-day moral theology, as well as remaining very attentive to the discoveries of biblical exegesis, has insisted on listening to the whole range of modern human sciences: biology, psychoanalysis, sociology, ethnology and the rest. I have the impression that in the process most weight has been given to the contributions of psychoanalysis, with a resulting imbalance in some theological writing. There are two well-known pitfalls in the use of psychoanalysis in ethics. One is to over-value the word and so to obscure the physiological basis of sexual behaviour, and the other is to encourage an inward-looking ethics and not to pay sufficient attention to the social dimensions of sexual life. But despite these problems it must be recognised that the use of these new anthropological understandings has enabled moral theology to make considerable progress. It has helped it to go beyond the often outmoded anthropology which used to underpin it and to ask new questions of scripture and tradition, and it has also made possible a new, realistic and more human approach in pastoral work. It is against this background that we shall examine a number of points which illustrate the operation of this mutual questioning of the human sciences and moral theology in the field of sexual ethics.

1. THE PLACE OF GENITAL ACTIVITY IN SEXUALITY

First, recent anthropology has shown that sexuality covers a much vaster area than genital activity alone. Biology just as much as psychological studies has enabled us to see that sexuality, far from being limited to the functioning of the genital organs, marks each human cell and underlies each human desire. In this sense sexuality is the masculine or feminine dimension which informs the whole reality of the individual from the first moments of his or her existence. It is now out of the question for a theologian to over-value genital activity in considering the regulation of sexuality. This regulation is not primarily a matter of the control of genital acts (masturbation and intercourse), but of a coming to terms in a human way with the sexual desires on which every human relationship is based. This broader conception of sexuality has also enabled moral theology to rediscover the importance of one scriptural teaching which had been ignored for far too long, the relational function of sexuality. The oldest creation story (Gen. 2) presents sexuality not primarily as having a procreative function, but as intended to rescue man from his unhealthy solitude. Chastity, the importance of which is stressed by the whole Christian tradition, will therefore in the future have to be carefully distinguished from continence (abstinence from orgasmic pleasures). Chastity must be understood as the virtue which enables an individual to make a fully humanising use of his or her sexual dimension, not only in his or her relations with others, but also in relating to the cosmos and God. Present-day moral theology, therefore, when it questions our contemporaries about their sexual lives, does not press them simply to assess the quality of their genital life; it asks them to relocate that life in the totality of their sexual life. To do this involves questions of this type: 'What use have I made of my various powers of seduction? Has this use promoted the freedom of others or has it ensnared them in my desires? Has my way of enjoying the elements of the cosmos been a way of settling into a regression or has it instead been a way of momentarily forgetting inadequacy in order to cope better with the inevitable frustrations of life? Is my relationship to God used to obscure my male or female dimension and to saturate my desire, or do I live it in such a way as to purify my desire as a man or woman and plumb its depths?'

2. THE LAW OF SYMBOLIC CASTRATION

The reader will have realised that ideas such as this reflect the influence on ethics of another modern anthropological contribution which has made possible a fresh approach to certain biblical narratives: I mean the importance of the law of castration for the emergence of the human individual. It is well known that anthropologists regard the transition from the state of the *infans* (etymologically: 'a creature incapable of speech') to the state of an active human individual capable of speaking and communicating as taking place through the imposition of a prohibition or law of separation, essentially the law of language. This law enables human young to escape from the 'tohu-bohu' of fusion with their origin and to breach the enclosure of imagination (with the desire for omnipotence which characterises it) in order to reach what is known as the symbolic order in which recognition of the other in his or her otherness can take place. Castration by the law therefore enables the individual to break the 'incestuous' (*in-castus*) tie with his or her origin in order to establish chaste (*casti*) ties which are always ways of integrating an insuperable and formative inadequacy. Chastity thought of in these terms is what makes possible a use of sexuality in which confusion is banished, that is to say, in which the human connection is underpinned by a proper articulation of otherness and identity.

This anthropological contribution has made it possible to re-read various passages of scripture in a new way. We have now seen, for example, that God's creative activity in

Genesis was presented as the establishment, on the basis of an original 'tohu-bohu', of an order in which the Word is a force for separation and a source of differentiation (Gen. 1), in which desire appears through the imposition of a prohibition (Gen. 2), and in which finally the recognition of the resemblance between man and God and between man and woman is possible because there is at the same time an acceptance of the differences between creature and creator and between the different elements of the created world. In the same way, the rules of purity in Leviticus 18–20 which concern sexuality can be understood as the expression of the wish not to sow confusion in the differentiated order of creation by means of realities which seem to obliterate boundaries (losses of blood or sperm, homosexuality, etc.)

In this way present-day moral theology sets at the heart of the notion of chastity a very modern idea, that of differentiation, seen as a destruction of the constantly reviving desire to reconstitute the lost fullness of the origin. In the end the great ethical question is how the human individual lives the dialectic of otherness and identity in the area of the three functions which scripture and anthropology attribute to sexuality. We will therefore examine how the moralist looks at the exercise of these functions.

3. CHASTITY AND THE THREE FUNCTIONS OF SEXUALITY

(a) The relational function

In relationships does the individual avoid both indifference (the denial of similarity) and indifferentiation (the rejection of otherness)? Is the partner experienced as an object fulfilling a need or as a mysterious subject extending the limits of desire? Is the loved one recognised as fallible, or does he or she reinforce the imaginary need of idealisation? Does the relationship allow for the time each partner takes to develop, or does it operate in the dream of all all at once, which is always the sign of the undue influence of primary narcissism. Is the difference resulting from the femininity or masculinity of the other accepted or rejected? It will be obvious that all these questions apply to everyone, whatever their social state (celibate, married, cohabiting, divorced, widowed) and even their psycho-sexual make-up (homosexuality, various forms of immaturity).

(b) The erotic function

This function is not absent from the Bible (see the Song of Solomon), but it has been the object of undue suspicion on the part of tradition. It has been restored to its proper importance by modern sexology and changing customs, and theology now takes account of it in its discussion, but subjects it, like the previous function, to the criterion of chastity understood as the proper regulation of the dialectic of difference and identity. Erotic pleasure is perhaps one of the phenomena which confront human beings most sharply with this dialectic. The pleasure is always an experience of identity because it is a momentary forgetting of the otherness of time and because it is a fleeting coincidence with oneself and with the other, who is the source of the pleasure. In this sense it is always a temporary forgetting of the inadequacy created by symbolic castration and so the reactualisation of an archaic phase of existence. That is why it is so easily sacralised: it fascinates and frightens at the same time because, while giving omnipotence and fusion, it is also the reactivation of a dangerous stage of indifferentiation. Nevertheless the pleasure is, paradoxically, at the same time an experience of the other. The pleasure makes the body feel other than the will in so far as the latter experiences itself as no longer in complete control. It is also an existential experience of dependence on the other, who is the source of the pleasure and demands a degree of self-abandonment. One of theology's tasks is therefore to indicate the way towards a proper regulation of pleasure by exposing the two contrary temptations inherent in it. As an experience of sameness, it may tend to be an escape from the other. This happens when an individual accumulates an unlimited succession of pleasures in an attempt to reconstitute the lost fullness of the world in the beginning. On the other hand, the experience of the other may drive an individual to refuse self-abandonment and freeze into an unreal asceticism which is in essence a sign of a desire to have total control over the other. Suspicion of pleasure has thus become, in the eyes of contemporary moralists, just as unhealthy as unrestrained pursuit of it.

(c) The procreative function

This function, which has been over-emphasised by tradition and the Church, but it can also be examined from the point of view of the dialectic of difference and identity. The child, the product of the sexual difference of the parents, is nonetheless of the same flesh as they. It therefore reawakens in them the imaginary dreams which slumber in them. The desire for a child may therefore be primarily the expression of a narcissistic wish to fill the emptiness within every human individual. Refusal to have a child, on the other hand, may be the expression of a refusal to confront the otherness of a being whom we know to be destined to escape from the grip of its parents. Paternity and maternity, in other words, are very often marked by a fundamental ambivalence.

4. SEXUALITY AS HISTORY

These considerations lead naturally to a third idea introduced by anthropological theory, namely that sexual behaviour is generally overdetermined, that is 'that it is related to a variety of unconscious elements which may be organised into different units of meaning, each of which, at a certain level of interpretation, has its own coherence'.[1] Moral theologians must therefore not let themselves be fascinated by the outward appearances of sexual behaviour. Outwardly it may appear wholly in conformity with the demands of the Word of God and be in fact a symptom of underlying attitudes which have very little to do with true humanity. For example, some forms of marital fidelity may be the sign of obsessional neurosis, some examples of continence may be due to a search for omnipotence; some refusals to enter into a permanent commitment which are presented as an expression of freedom may in fact be expressions of excessive attachment to the mother, etc. In contrast, it is possible that in the history of a particular individual the rejection of an evangelical demand may be an attempt to attain a more human sexual life. For example, a particular young person's refusal to marry may be an important stage of distancing from over-possessive parental authority. Moral theology thus makes ethical judgments more complex by including the individual's unconscious and history as crucial elements of discernment. In this way sexual ethics is following the general thrust of modern philosophy in distancing itself from the a-historical approach of classical anthropology.

However, this introduction of history into the field of sexuality is not limited to a restoration of an individual's sexual behaviour to the context of his or her developing awareness. It also takes the form of a new way of understanding sexuality itself. Modern studies, notably those of Freud, show that sexuality is not a monolithic, static instinct, set in place once and for all at the end of adolescence, but that it has and even is a history. Far from being static, an individual's sexual make-up is a system more or less subject to a variety of partial pressures. In other words, moral theology should think of sexuality as of course something partly capable of being regulated by the human will, but also as something which develops independently in a process over which consciousness often has very little control. Moralists should now accept that there is no such thing as perfect sexuality, and that complete control does not exist in sexual life any more than it does in the other areas of existence. It is in the nature of sexuality to be marked by failures, regressions, continuance in immature stages and compulsive moments just as much as by moments of pleasure and joy, maturing and sublimation in freedom. This complex situation makes many demands on moral theology.

First of all it must make a careful distinction between what is the result of sinful will and what is the expression of human finitude; this is the basis of any healthy conception of sin in the area of sex.

It must also take full account of atypical psycho-sexual make-ups, which for the individual as he or she has developed in the course of his or her history, are nonetheless definitive. There are millions of human beings around the world who are incapable of realising all the dimensions of sexuality—relational, erotic and psychological—because they are fixed in a particular sexual orientation such as homosexuality or affected by orgasmic and/or relational inhibitions underlying their desires. Moreover, these people are often incapable of achieving continence or, if they do, often do so at the cost of genuine pleasure in life. This is one of the most difficult problems and most important tasks of moral theology. How can it help these 'atypical' people to find moral guidelines which will allow them, without being crushed by 'heavy burdens', to regulate their genital and sexual lives as well as possible? It seems to me that in this area theological research has so far made little progress, a fact which is easily understood when we allow for another contribution of sexual anthropology to which I now wish to turn, its interest in the systemic and socio-cultural dimension of sex.

5. THE SYSTEMIC AND SOCIO-CULTURAL DIMENSION OF SEXUALITY

Ethical treatments in the past were often inadequate because of an excessively 'substantialist' attitude, which regarded actions as isolated and independent. For example, there would be discussions of masturbation in general as an intrinsically perverted act or of cohabitation in general as a sexual relationship outside marriage which was radically opposed to the plan of God. One of the most characteristic recent developments in moral theology has been to situate the 'substantialist' approach within a systemic view. Now moral theologians see sexual behaviour as part of systems, that is, sets of elements which interact with each other. Specifically, this means that an individual's sexual behaviour does not have meaning in itself, but only in the synchronic distances between it and the other elements of the system to which it belongs. An individual's sexuality forms a system with the individual's relation to aggression, money, the dominant ideology, the social class to which he or she belongs, etc. Consequently, when moral theologians consider a particular sexual question such as cohabitation, they fall into an error of method if they treat it from an exclusively interior and sexological point of view. That is why ethical study of sexuality begins by setting up a typology of forms of behaviour, which shows that there is not in fact a single phenomenon of masturbation, but acts of masturbation, not a single situation of cohabitation outside marriage, but a variety of relationships whose individual and social significance is by no means identical. Ethical consideration thus becomes the art of grasping the interactions, of perceiving realities as organised and complex wholes, of discerning the movement of systems in an attempt to discover the point to which they are leading societies. This discernment must draw on two sources, both of which are indispensable, the analystic techniques of the social sciences and Christian tradition, which exercises an important critical function. I shall explain.

G

6. THE CRITICAL FUNCTION OF TRADITION

The ethical norms of tradition are in fact the historical traces of the responses given by the Christians of the past to the problem of achieving self-fulfilment as free human beings through submission to the lordship of Christ. Because these responses of our predecessors were made in situations totally different from our own, the norms must be treated as relative. But in so far as they indicate the direction in which our Christian ancestors looked for the actualisation of their relationship with God, they should be treated as a summons to our memory to help us to understand the present and so enable us to invent a more human future. And certainly, when we find that an ethical rule relating to a form of behaviour of profound human significance has been constantly and universally maintained by tradition, it is then highly probable that that rule embodies many essential values. Breaking that rule thus means being unfaithful to the Word of God. Christian tradition has a number of rules relating to sexuality which can help theologians not to be the victim of the dominant social stereotypes and, more positively, enable them to challenge their contemporaries with serenity.

Among these rules the very first which in my view should be re-emphasised is that of marital fidelity and the value of a definitive commitment. Our society is experiencing an increasing instability in sexual relationships. It is as if the principles of management applied to financial capital have been transposed to sexual desire. In this framework fidelity is seen primarily as the optimal realisation of a capital (desire) invested in whichever relationship at the moment brings the fastest return. Familiarity with the Word of God protects the moralist from sinking into such an 'economistic' view of human relationships. Tradition shows us that sexuality is not an energy to be used but a mystery involving the whole person which attains its full dimension only when it is confronted in *agape* with the otherness of the other sex, a process which takes time.

The sacramental theology which regards love as a practical parable of God's unfailing love for human beings enables us to understand better that there can be no real conjugal love which does not take the risk of a permanent commitment. Making a permanent commitment is a profound act of faith in the other person because it means a desire to receive oneself in part from them. In this way, to take up what was said earlier about the dialectic of difference and identity, fidelity and the word given for life represent attempts to escape from the total control of identity in order to abandon oneself partly to difference. In this sense, if they are not perverted, they are signs of a true chastity, that is of a true symbolic castration of the imaginary dream of immediacy.

Another norm constantly upheld by moral theology may be a useful source of questions for our contemporaries, that of the necessity of an institution within which love is made real. Love does not exhaust its meaning in the intimacy of a relationship; it also possesses a radical social dimension. Moralists today must therefore try to get across something that is no longer obvious to many young people, namely that the institutional aspect can be experienced as an opportunity. It is an opportunity to take seriously the finitude of human beings, whose freedom to develop needs other people, social rules and regulation by rites. It is an opportunity to insert human desire effectively into social space by eliminating its excess of individuality.

I shall conclude by mentioning one of the most fundamental norms theology finds in its past: the evangelical relativisation of every human bond in the face of the only Absolute, God. Putting such a norm into practice helps to take some of the obsessiveness out of all sexual attachments (Luke 18:29). This may be a question to be put to Western societies which, in the opinion of many sociologists, have exaggerated expectations of the couple and the child, and ultimately of sexuality. This question could be formulated as follows: 'Remember that no sexual attachment leads to development unless, over time, it opens itself in welcome to the kingdom, and one of the most important signs of this is effective, practical solidarity with the humble and poor of this world.'

Translated by Francis McDonagh

Note

1. Laplanche, J., and Pontalis *Vocabulaire de la psychanalyse* (Paris 1971) p. 467.

Barbara Andolsen

Loyal Dissent of the Faithful: Report from USA

THE CATHOLIC Church's teachings on sexuality provide guidance, not just on the morality of genital activity, but more broadly about how one ought to live as male or female in the world. The Church bases its teaching on a stable model of man and woman, each endowed by the Creator with special physical and psychological characteristics. This model is a heterosexual model. For the sexually active, the Catholic Church provides a single ideal of chastity. Human sexuality is put to proper use when a married couple, open to the possibility of conceiving a child, have intercourse which culminates in the ejaculation of the husband's seminal fluid in the vagina of his wife.

In the United States,[1] many Catholics perceive a tension between their daily experience and the Church's teachings. I will discuss three of the forms it takes: (1) Catholic mothers who work for wages find that responsibilities for home and children plus obligations at work are a heavy burden. (2) Married couples, facing serious economic pressures and desirous of mutual support and growth, believe that they can responsibly remain open to the conception of a child relatively few times during their married life. (3) Persons with a permanent homosexual orientation desire to express love physically with partners of the same sex. However, for such persons, the unitive and procreative aspects of sexuality are permanently separated.

1. DUTIES OF MOTHERS AND FATHERS

Twentieth-century papal teachings about human sexuality have presupposed a complementarity of the sexes. This complementarity is not merely physical, but also one of temperament. Men have traits such as rationality and leadership which make them fit to oversee order in the home and in the world. Women are endowed with traits such as warmth, religious fervour, and sensitivity to the feelings and needs of others. Women's traits carry with them a special obligation to provide comfort for others and especially to care for children.

Recent popes have agreed that motherhood defines a woman's nature. John XXIII told a papal audience that 'the end for which the Creator fashioned woman's whole being is motherhood. This vocation to motherhood is . . . so much a part of her nature that it is operative even when actual generation does not occur.'[2] Even women who do not bear children are encouraged to find motherly vocations (teaching, nursing, etc.) or to approach less traditional callings with a distinctive female sensitivity.

John XXIII explicitly recognised that women were working outside the home in increasing numbers and that women valued economic independence. He knew the difficulties facing families where both spouses worked. He recognised that work could be boring and dehumanising; that people look to the home as a warm and loving environment in which their energies are restored. But who is to create this restorative environment when both spouses work? John XXIII answered, 'Here again, there is a great task waiting for women: let them promise themselves that they will not let their contacts with the harsh realities of outside work dry up . . . the resources of their sensitivity, of their open and delicate spirit. . . .'[3] John XXIII believed that only women possessed those personality traits essential for creating a warm, peaceful home. Therefore, working women should assume most of the household responsibilities.

While John Paul II thinks society should give mothers the option of remaining at home, he seems to have fully accepted the fact that women often work outside the home. He insists that society should allow women to participate in the workplace without discrimination. However, women's work should be organised to permit them to fulfill their duties as wives and mothers. For 'women as mothers have an irreplacable role'[4] in the family.

John Paul II has not been specific about the social changes necessary for women to fulfill their responsibilities as mothers without being penalised as workers. Nor has he mentioned the 'irreplacable role' of men as fathers in the development of their children. He demands that women should not be required to 'pay for their [job] advancement . . . at the expense of the family'.[5] However, he has not articulated the same demand for men.

The Church has said little about the concrete social conditions which make it difficult for wage earning women to meet their obligations to their families. In the United States, the majority of families include a woman who works outside the home. Almost one-half of the women who have children *under six* are working for wages. Sociological studies show that women who work full-time also put in long hours in housework and child care. One study reviewing fifty years of data on housework concluded that 'for married women in full time jobs the work day is probably longer than it was for their grandmothers [on the farm]'.[6] Other studies in the United States and in Europe confirm that men spend few hours in household work. Men whose wives work for wages perform only a few more household tasks than do men whose wives do not work outside the home.

Church leaders have rarely spoken about the man's responsibility to create a warm, loving home. Paul VI did say that 'it is desirable that both father and mother collaborate in raising and educating the children and there is certainly room for men to make a greater contribution'. However, he emphasised woman's role more strongly. 'Yet the woman's role is evidently essential.'[7] Church teachings about the duties of mothers and fathers are a part of its understanding about how persons live responsibly as male and female. Some Catholic women and men reject the Church's differential standard for mothers and fathers and urge a more egalitarian family ethic.

2. BIRTH CONTROL

In the teachings of the Church, the complementarity of the sexes in society mirrors their physical complementarity. Male and female are created for the purpose of procreation. At Vatican II the bishops spoke eloquently about the unitive function of marital intercourse. No longer is procreation seen as the sole primary end of marriage. Nonetheless, the sexual organs are seen as designed by God for reproduction. Any use of the sexual organs in a manner which artificially impedes the procreative function is condemned. 'Each and every marriage act must remain open to the transmission of life.'[8]

Many commentators have criticised such Church statements for a reductionist physicalism that abstracts human reproductive capacities from all other capacities of the human person and from the social relationships in which persons use their sexual organs. Official Church commentaries also reflect male physical experience. After puberty, most men are fertile for the rest of their lives. For most men full sexual release (orgasm) is accompanied by a release of sperm. Therefore, for many males, genital activity has a direct biological link to procreative potential.

In women's bodily experience, however, procreation and sexual release are not so closely linked. After puberty, women are fertile for only a portion of their adult lives. Women release ova according to a biological cycle unrelated to genital activity. Unlike many animals, human females do not limit their sexual contact to their fertile period. Many women remain sexually active for a significant time after menopause. Women have a sexual organ with no direct procreative function: the clitoris. Women's sexual pleasure has no essential physiological connection with procreation. If theologians reflected seriously on the physical experience of women, it is doubtful that they could conclude that procreation is *the* end of female sexuality.

It is well known that many married Catholics dissent from the Church's position on birth control. Moreover, this dissent is of long standing. One study has shown that Catholic women in the United States were using artificial birth control in significant numbers even before the Second Vatican Council.[9] Studies at Princeton University have shown that over 80 percent of American Catholic women who are limiting births are using a means other than rhythm. The use of rhythm as a method for birth control is declining steadily, especially among younger women. Research suggests that even greater deviation from the Church's teaching can be expected in the future.[10]

Some couples who use artificial means of birth control are motivated by selfishness or an excessive desire for material goods. However, other couples believe that they are making a responsible moral decision. Hard economic times make financial pressures on couples, especially poorer couples, particularly severe. Many couples judge that they must restrict births in order to provide adequate economic, emotional, and spiritual support for the children they already have.

An increasing number of women who work for wages find that the double burden of workplace and home responsibilities makes it impossible to mother more than a few children adequately. The Church's plea for an economic system that would allow mothers to remain at home would not solve this problem entirely. Women will continue to work because they draw personal as well as financial benefits from work. An increasing number of women find that work outside the home allows them to 'fulfill that calling to be a person that is . . . [theirs] by reason of . . . [their] very humanity'.[11]

Sexual intercourse is an important bond in the union of most married couples, as Vatican II recognised. Most American Catholic couples believe that the use of a reliable means of artificial birth control is the best way to preserve the good of their sexual communion while conceiving only those children for whom they can responsibly care. Many of the faithful struggling to live morally upright lives assert that the use of birth control enhances, and does not diminish their married life.

The gulf between official teaching and personal practice concerning birth control is widely known. In his statement to the 1980 Synod of Bishops, Archbishop John Quinn of San Francisco reported that many Catholic couples 'whose lives are otherwise outstanding in their Christian dedication'[12] use artificial means of birth control. When the experience of the faithful and Church teachings are so fundamentally opposed, a crisis of moral authority exists.

3. HOMOSEXUALITY

Birth control is condemned because it divorces sexual intercourse from its life-giving dimension. The Church also condemns homosexual activity because it cannot be procreative.[13] Church officials condemn homosexual activity not only because it violates the physical complementarity of the sexes, but also because it challenges the psychological complementarity of male and female. (This latter argument is made explicitly only in the writings of theologians in agreement with the *magisterium*). United States theologian Edward Malloy, has argued that homosexual unions are disordered because they lack the potential for life-time fidelity. He claims lesbian and homosexual partners inevitably become bored with one another, because of gender similarity. Then, they separate. 'It seems that only the mystery of the other, especially when rooted in gender specificity can sustain the ongoing task of self-giving and mutual domestic responsibility.'[14] Canadian theologian André Guindon develops a sexual ethic based upon an analysis of sexuality as a language for dialogue. The sexual dialogue is only genuine when it is communion between two fundamentally different persons—a woman and a man. '. . . the homosexual relationship fails as a totally human relationship. The authentic human sense of the other, as nourished by the enriching and complementary otherness of the other sex, is conspicuously absent. The other side of the bed is occupied, as it were, only by more of the same.'[15]

There is contemporary sociological evidence that connects strict gender role expectations and condemnation of homosexual behaviour. One study of US college students showed students who had traditional views about male and female behaviour also disapproved of homosexual conduct.[16] Another United States' study showed: 'Some people condemned the homosexual person, whom they erroneously believed to be feminine when male, and masculine when female. Any threat to the traditional masculine-feminine dichotomy was abhorred.'[17] Similar attitudes have been found in Canada and Brazil.

It is difficult to discuss the experience of homosexual Catholics. Since the Church and society condemn homosexuality and stigmatise it as unnatural, many lesbians and homosexual men conceal their true experience. Indeed, in societies which teach people from earliest childhood that heterosexual relationships are normative, it is difficult for some persons to acknowledge a homosexual orientation, even to themselves. Thus, we cannot assume that all homosexual persons are like those most visible to the media or even to social scientists.

Both sociological studies and anecdotal reports discuss the multiple sex partners of homosexual men. Studies of lesbian women, on the other hand, are more likely to show they have only one partner or few partners over the course of many years. The lack of fidelity to a single sex partner, particularly among homosexual males, may be related to a lack of social structures—including spiritual structures—which would support long-lasting homosexual or lesbian relationships. However, there are homosexual and lesbian couples who have loving relationships of many years duration, but who are reluctant to speak publicly about their experience because of social disapproval.

Some lesbians and homosexual men regret their homosexual orientation and would prefer to be heterosexual. These persons tend to have difficulty establishing satisfying, long-lasting sexual partnerships. Other homosexual men and lesbians, accept themselves as they are. They assert that coming to terms with their sexual orientation enhances their emotional maturity, honesty, and openness to others. Some lesbian women say that to choose to love another woman is a sign of healthy self-acceptance as a woman, as well as love for the other. Since most societies teach women that they are inherently inferior creatures, self-love is no small moral accomplishment for a woman. This is not to suggest that a lesbian relationship is the only context in which a woman can affirm the goodness of her own being as a woman. However, some lesbians report they achieve such a liberating self-affirmation through a sexual love for another woman.

Many homosexual or lesbian couples speak eloquently of the deep friendship which they experience with their partners. Some lesbian women say pointedly that their relationships are marked by an equality between the partners that a male and female pair finds nearly impossible to achieve within present social structures. A homosexual or lesbian couple cannot conceive a child as a result of their own love making. But they insist that their relationship can be life sustaining and socially enriching in many other ways. Since procreation is not a possibility in homosexual relationships, such relationships force theologians to reflect upon sexual activity engaged in purely for mutual bonding and reciprocal pleasure. Homosexual men and lesbian women claim that sexual activity is valuable for those purposes alone.

The Church's official teachings on sexuality depend upon a model of men and women as physically and psychologically different and as inevitably oriented toward heterosexual encounters. The experience of Catholic men and women is far more diverse. As long as the Catholic Church maintains this solitary paradigm of human sexuality, there will continue to be a serious gap between the practice of some conscientious members and the official teachings of the Church.

Notes

1. This article will concentrate on the experience of the faithful in the United States. This is the culture which my experience and research best qualify me to describe.

2. John XXIII 'Address to Several Italian Women's Associations' 6 September 1961, *Pope Speaks* 7 (1961) p. 345.

3. John XXIII 'Address to the Italian Centre for Women' 7 December 1960, *Pope Speaks* 7 (1961) p. 172.

4. John Paul II *Laborem Exercens* ¶ 19.

5. *Ibid.*

6. J. Vanek 'Time Spent in Housework' *Scientific American* November 1974, 120.

7. Paul VI 'Address to the Study Commission on Women' 31 January 1976, *Pope Speaks* 21 (1976) p. 164.

8. Paul VI *Humanae Vitae* ¶ 11.

9. C. Westoff and L. Bumpass 'The Revolution in Birth Control Practices of U.S. Catholics' *Science*, 179 (1973) 42.

10. C. Westoff and N. Ryder *The Contraceptive Revolution* (Princeton 1977) 23–27.

11. John Paul II *Laborem Exercens* ¶ 6.

12. Contraception; a Proposal for the Synod, *Catholic Mind* 79 (1981) 27.

13. Condemnations of homosexual activity are also based on scriptural teachings which cannot be discussed in this brief essay.

14. E. Malloy *Homosexuality and the Christian Way of Life* (Washington 1981) p. 234.

15. A. Guindon *The Sexual Language* (Ottawa 1976) 339.

16. N. Henley and F. Pincus 'Interrelationship of Sexist, Racist, and Antihomosexual Attitudes' *Psychology Reports* 42 (1978) pp. 83–90.

17. J. Gramick 'Prejudice, Religion and Homosexual People' in *A Challenge to Love* ed. R. Nugent (New York 1983) 7.

Sacred Congregation for the Doctrine of the Faith

Documentation: Declaration on Certain Questions Concerning Sexual Ethics

1. According to contemporary scientific research, the human person is so profoundly affected by sexuality that it must be considered as one of the factors which give to each individual's life the principal traits that distinguish it. In fact it is from sex that the human person receives the characteristics which, on the biological, psychological and spiritual levels, make that person a man or a woman, and thereby largely condition his or her progress towards maturity and insertion into society. Hence sexual matters, as is obvious to everyone, today constitute a theme frequently and openly dealt with in books, reviews, magazines and other means of social communication.

In the present period, the corruption of morals has increased, and one of the most serious indications of this corruption is the unbridled exaltation of sex. Moreover, through the means of social communication and through public entertainment this corruption has reached the point of invading the field of education and of infecting the general mentality.

In this context certain educators, teachers and moralists have been able to contribute to a better understanding and integration into life of the values proper to each of the sexes; on the other hand there are those who have put forward concepts and modes of behaviour which are contrary to the true moral exigencies of the human person. Some members of the latter group have even gone so far as to favour a licentious hedonism.

As a result, in the course of a few years, teachings, moral criteria and modes of living hitherto faithfully preserved have been very much unsettled, even among Christians. There are many people today who, being confronted with so many widespread opinions opposed to the teaching which they received from the Church, have come to wonder what they must still hold as true.

2. The Church cannot remain indifferent to this confusion of minds and relaxation of morals. It is a question, in fact, of a matter which is of the utmost importance both for the personal lives of Christians and for the social life of our time.[1]

The Bishops are daily led to note the growing difficulties experienced by the faithful in obtaining knowledge of wholesome moral teaching, especially in sexual matters, and of the growing difficulties experienced by pastors in expounding this teaching effectively. The Bishops know that by their pastoral charge they are called upon to meet the needs of their faithful in this very serious matter, and important documents dealing with it have already been published by some of them or by Episcopal Conferences. Nevertheless, since the erroneous opinions and resulting deviations are continuing to spread everywhere, the Sacred Congregation for the Doctrine of the Faith, by virtue of its function in the universal Church[2] and by a mandate of the Supreme Pontiff, has judged it necessary to publish the present Declaration.

3. The people of our time are more and more convinced that the human person's dignity and vocation demand that they should discover, by the light of their own intelligence, the values innate in their nature, that they should ceaselessly develop these values and realize them in their lives, in order to achieve an ever greater development.

In moral matters man cannot make value judgments according to his personal whim: 'In the depths of his conscience, man detects a law which he does not impose on himself, but which holds him to obedience . . . For man has in his heart a law written by God. To obey it is the very dignity of man; according to it he will be judged.'[3]

Moreover, through his revelation God has made known to us Christians his plan of salvation, and he has held up to us Christ, the Saviour and Sanctifier, in his teaching and example, as the supreme and immutable Law of life: 'I am the light of the world; anyone who follows me will not be walking in the dark, he will have the light of life.'[4]

Therefore there can be no true promotion of man's dignity unless the essential order of his nature is respected. Of course, in the history of civilisation many of the concrete conditions and needs of human life have changed and will continue to change. But all evolution of morals and every type of life must be kept within the limits imposed by the immutable principles based upon every human person's constitutive elements and essential relations—elements and relations which transcend historical contingency.

These fundamental principles, which can be grasped by reason, are contained in 'the divine law—eternal, objective and universal—whereby God orders, directs and governs the entire universe and all the ways of the human community, by a plan conceived in wisdom and love. Man has been made by God to participate in this law, with the result that, under the gentle disposition of divine Providence, he can come to perceive ever increasingly the unchanging truth'.[5] This divine law is accessible to our minds.

4. Hence, those many people are in error who today assert that one can find neither in human nature nor in the revealed law any absolute and immutable norm to serve for particular actions other than the one which expresses itself in the general law of charity and respect for human dignity. As a proof of their assertion they put forward the view that so-called norms of the natural law or precepts of Sacred Scripture are to be regarded only as given expressions of a form of particular culture at a certain moment of history.

But in fact, divine Revelation and, in its own proper order philosophical wisdom, emphasize the authentic exigencies of human nature. They thereby necessarily manifest the existence of immutable laws inscribed in the constitutive elements of human nature and which are revealed to be identical in all beings endowed with reason.

Furthermore, Christ instituted his Church as 'the pillar and bulwark of truth'.[6] With the Holy Spirit's assistance, she ceaselessly preserves and transmits without error the truths of the moral order, and she authentically interprets not only the revealed positive law but 'also . . . those principles of the moral order which have their origin in human nature itself'[7] and which concern man's full development and sanctification. Now in fact the Church throughout her history has always considered a certain number of precepts of the natural law as having an absolute and immutable value, and in their transgression she has seen a contradiction of the teaching and spirit of the Gospel.

5. Since sexual ethics concern certain fundamental values of human and Christian life, this general teaching equally applies to sexual ethics. In this domain there exist principles and norms which the Church has always unhesitatingly transmitted as part of her teaching, however much the opinions and morals of the world may have been opposed to

them. These principles and norms in no way owe their origin to a certain type of culture, but rather to knowledge of the divine law and of human nature. They therefore cannot be considered as having become out of date or doubtful under the pretext that a new cultural situation has arisen.

It is these principles which inspired the exhortations and directives given by the Second Vatican Council for an education and organisation of social life taking account of the equal dignity of man and woman while respecting their difference.[8]

Speaking of 'the sexual nature of man and the human faculty of procreation', the Council noted that they 'wonderfully exceed the dispositions of lower forms of life'.[9] It then took particular care to expound the principles and criteria which concern human sexuality in marriage, and which are based upon the finality of the specific function of sexuality.

In this regard the Council declares that the moral goodness of the acts proper to conjugal life, acts which are ordered according to true human dignity, 'does not depend solely on sincere intentions or on an evaluation of motives. It must be determined by objective standards. These, based on the nature of the human person and his acts, preserve the full sense of mutual self-giving and human procreation in the context of true love'.[10]

These final words briefly sum up the Council's teaching—more fully expounded in an earlier part of the same Constitution[11]—on the finality of the sexual act and on the principal criterion of its morality: it is respect for its finality that ensures the moral goodness of this act.

This same principle, which the Church holds from divine Revelation and from her authentic interpretation of the natural law, is also the basis of her traditional doctrine, which states that the use of the sexual function has its true meaning and moral rectitude only in true marriage.[12]

6. It is not the purpose of the present Declaration to deal with all the abuses of the sexual faculty, nor with all the elements involved in the practice of chastity. Its object is rather to repeat the Church's doctrine on certain particular points, in view of the urgent need to oppose serious errors and widespread aberrant modes of behaviour.

7. Today there are many who vindicate the right to sexual union before marriage, at least in those cases where a firm intention to marry and an affection which is already in some way conjugal in the psychology of the subjects require this completion, which they judge to be con-natural. This is especially the case when the celebration of the marriage is impeded by circumstances or when this intimate relationship seems necessary in order for love to be preserved.

This opinion is contrary to Christian doctrine, which states that every genital act must be within the framework of marriage. However firm the intention of those who practise such premature sexual relations may be, the fact remains that these relations cannot ensure, in sincerity and fidelity, the interpersonal relationship between a man and a woman, nor especially can they protect this relationship from whims and caprices. Now it is a stable union that Jesus willed, and he restored its original requirement, beginning with the sexual difference. 'Have you not read that the creator from the beginning made them male and female and that he said: This is why a man must leave father and mother, and cling to his wife, and the two become one body? They are no longer two, therefore, but one body. So then, what God has united, man must not divide.'[13] Saint Paul will be even more explicit when he shows that if unmarried people or widows cannot live chastely they have no other alternative than the stable union of marriage: '. . . it is better to marry than to be aflame with passion.'[14] Through marriage, in fact, the love of married people is taken up into that love which Christ irrevocably has for the Church,[15] while dissolute sexual union[16] defiles the temple of the Holy Spirit which the Christian has become. Sexual union therefore is only legitimate if a definitive community of life has been established between the man and the woman.

This is what the Church has always understood and taught,[17] and she finds a profound agreement with her doctrine in men's reflection and in the lessons of history.

Experience teaches us that love must find its safeguard in the stability of marriage, if sexual intercourse is truly to respond to the requirements of its own finality and to those of human dignity. These requirements call for a conjugal contract sanctioned and guaranteed by society—a contract which establishes a state of life of capital importance both for the exclusive union of the man and the woman and for the good of their family and of the human community. Most often, in fact, pre-marital relations exclude the possibility of children. What is represented to be conjugal love is not able, as it absolutely should be, to develop into paternal and maternal love. Or, if it does happen to do so, this will be to the detriment of the children, who will be deprived of the stable environment in which they ought to develop in order to find in it the way and the means of their insertion into society as a whole.

The consent given by people who wish to be united in marriage must therefore be manifested externally and in a manner which makes it valid in the eyes of society. As far as the faithful are concerned, their consent to the setting up of a community of conjugal life must be expressed according to the laws of the Church. It is a consent which makes their marriage a Sacrament of Christ.

8. At the present time there are those who, basing themselves on observations in the psychological order, have begun to judge indulgently, and even to excuse completely, homosexual relations between certain people. This they do in opposition to the constant teaching of the *Magisterium* and to the moral sense of the Christian people.

A distinction is drawn, and it seems with some reason, between homosexuals whose tendency comes from a false education, from a lack of normal sexual development, from habit, from bad example, or from other similar causes, and is transitory or at least not incurable; and homosexuals who are definitively such because of some kind of innate instinct or a pathological constitution judged to be incurable.

In regard to this second category of subjects, some people conclude that their tendency is so natural that it justifies in their case homosexual relations within a sincere communion of life and love analogous to marriage, in so far as such homosexuals feel incapable of enduring a solitary life.

In the pastoral field, these homosexuals must certainly be treated with understanding and sustained in the hope of overcoming their personal difficulties and their inability to fit into society. Their culpability will be judged with prudence. But no pastoral method can be employed which would give moral justification to these acts on the grounds that they would be consonant with the condition of such people. For according to the objective moral order, homosexual relations are acts which lack an essential and indispensable finality. In Sacred Scripture they are condemned as a serious depravity and even presented as the sad consequence of rejecting God.[18] This judgment of Scripture does not of course permit us to conclude that all those who suffer from this anomaly are personally responsible for it, but it does attest to the fact that homosexual acts are intrinsically disordered and can in no case be approved of.

9. The traditional Catholic doctrine that masturbation constitutes a grave moral disorder is often called into doubt or expressly denied today. It is said that psychology and sociology show that it is a normal phenomenon of sexual development, especially among the young. It is stated that there is real and serious fault only in the measure that the subject deliberately indulges in solitary pleasure closed in on self (ipsation), because in this case the act would indeed be radically opposed to the loving communion between persons of different sex which some hold is what is principally sought in the use of the sexual faculty.

This opinion is contradictory to the teaching and pastoral practice of the Catholic Church. Whatever the force of certain arguments of a biological and philosophical nature, which have sometimes been used by theologians, in fact both the *Magisterium* of the Church—in the course of a constant tradition—and the moral sense of the faithful have declared without hesitation that masturbation is an intrinsically and seriously disordered act.[19] The main reason is that, whatever the motive for acting in this way, the deliberate use of the sexual faculty outside normal conjugal relations essentially contradicts the finality of the faculty. For it lacks the sexual relationship called for by the moral order, namely the relationship which realizes 'the full sense of mutual self-giving and human procreation in the context of true love'.[20] All deliberate exercise of sexuality must be reserved to this regular relationship. Even if it cannot be proved that Scripture condemns this sin by name, the tradition of the Church has rightly understood it to be condemned in the New Testament when the latter speaks of 'impurity', 'unchasteness' and other vices contrary to chastity and continence.

Sociological surveys are able to show the frequency of this disorder according to the places, populations or circumstances studied. In this way facts are discovered, but facts do not constitute a criterion for judging the moral value of human acts.[21] The frequency of the phenomenon in question is certainly to be linked with man's innate weakness following original sin; but it is also to be linked with the loss of a sense of God, with the corruption of morals engendered by the commercialisation of vice, with the unrestrained licentiousness of so many public entertainments and publications, as well as with the neglect of modesty, which is the guardian of chastity.

On the subject of masturbation modern psychology provides much valid and useful information for formulating a more equitable judgment on moral responsibility and for orienting pastoral action. Psychology helps one to see how the immaturity of adolescence (which can sometimes persist after that age), psychological imbalance or habit can influence behaviour, diminishing the deliberate character of the act and bringing about a situation whereby subjectively there may not always be serious fault. But in general, the absence of serious responsibility must not be presumed; this would be to misunderstand people's moral capacity.

In the pastoral ministry, in order to form an adequate judgment in concrete cases, the habitual behaviour of people will be considered in its totality, not only with regard to the individual's practice of charity and of justice but also with regard to the individual's care in observing the particular precepts of chastity. In particular, one will have to examine whether the individual is using the necessary means, both natural and supernatural, which Christian asceticism from its long experience recommends for overcoming the passions and progressing in virtue.

10. The observance of the moral law in the field of sexuality and the practice of chastity have been considerably endangered, especially among less fervent Christians, by the current tendency to minimize as far as possible, when not denying outright, the reality of grave sin, at least in people's actual lives.

There are those who go as far as to affirm that mortal sin, which causes separation from God, only exists in the formal refusal directly opposed to God's call, or in that selfishness which completely and deliberately closes itself to the love of neighbour. They say that it is only then that there comes into play the fundamental option, that is to say the decision which totally commits the person and which is necessary if mortal sin is to exist; by this option the person, from the depths of the personality, takes up or ratifies a fundamental attitude towards God or people. On the contrary, so-called 'peripheral' actions (which, it is said, usually do not involve decisive choice), do not go so far as to change the fundamental option, the less so since they often come, as is observed, from habit. Thus such actions can weaken the fundamental option, but not to such a degree as to change it completely. Now according to these authors, a change of the fundamental option towards God less easily comes about in the field of sexual activity, where a person generally does not transgress the moral order in a fully deliberate and responsible manner but rather under the influence of passion, weakness, immaturity, sometimes even through the illusion of thus showing love for someone else. To these causes there is often added the pressure of the social environment.

In reality, it is precisely the fundamental option which in the last resort defines a person's moral disposition. But it can be completely changed by particular acts, especially when, as often happens, these have been prepared for by previous more superficial acts. Whatever the case, it is wrong to say that particular acts are not enough to constitute mortal sin.

According to the Church's teaching, mortal sin, which is opposed to God, does not consist only in formal and direct resistance to the commandment of charity. It is equally to be found in this opposition to authentic love which is included in every deliberate transgression, in serious matter, of each of the moral laws.

Christ himself has indicated the double commandment of love as the basis of the moral life. But on this commandment depends 'the whole Law, and the Prophets also'.[22] It therefore includes the other particular precepts. In fact, to the young man who asked, '. . . what good deed must I do to possess eternal life?' Jesus replied: '. . . if you wish to enter into life, keep the commandments . . . You must not kill. You must not commit adultery. You must not steal. You must not bring false witness. Honour your father and mother, and: you must love your neighbour as yourself.'[23]

A person therefore sins mortally not only when his action comes from direct contempt for love of God and neighbour, but also when he consciously and freely, for whatever reason, chooses something which is seriously disordered. For in this choice, as has been said above, there is already included contempt for the divine commandment: the person turns himself away from God and loses charity. Now according to Christian tradition and the Church's teaching, and as right reason also recognizes, the moral order of sexuality involves such high values of human life that every direct violation of this order is objectively serious.[24]

It is true that in sins of the sexual order, in view of their kind and their causes, it more easily happens that free consent is not fully given; this is a fact which calls for caution in all judgment as to the subject's responsibility. In this matter it is particularly opportune to recall the following words of Scripture: 'Man looks at appearances but God looks at the heart.'[25] However, although prudence is recommended in judging the subjective seriousness of a particular sinful act, it in no way follows that one can hold the view that in the sexual field mortal sins are not committed.

Pastors of souls must therefore exercise patience and goodness; but they are not allowed to render God's commandments null, nor to reduce unreasonably people's responsibility. 'To diminish in no way the saving teaching of Christ constitutes an eminent form of charity for souls. But this must ever be accompanied by patience and goodness, such as the Lord himself gave example of in dealing with people. Having come not to condemn but to save, he was indeed intransigent with evil, but merciful towards individuals.'[26]

11. As has been said above, the purpose of this Declaration is to draw the attention of the faithful in present-day circumstances to certain errors and modes of behaviour which they must guard against. The virtue of chastity, however, is in no way confined solely to avoiding the faults already listed. It is aimed at attaining higher and more positive goals. It is a virtue which concerns the whole personality, as regards both interior and outward behaviour.

Individuals should be endowed with this virtue according to their state in life: for some it will mean virginity or celibacy consecrated to God, which is an eminent way of giving oneself more easily to God alone with an undivided heart.[27] For others it will take the form determined by the moral law, according to whether they are married or single. But whatever the state of life, chastity is not simply an external state; it must make a person's heart pure in accordance with Christ's words: 'You have learned how it was said: You must not commit adultery. But I say this to you: if a man looks at a woman lustfully, he has already committed adultery with her in his heart.'[28]

Chastity is included in that continence which Saint Paul numbers among the gifts of the Holy Spirit, while he condemns sensuality as a vice particularly unworthy of the Christian and one which precludes entry into the kingdom of heaven.[29] 'What God wants is for all to be holy. He wants you to keep away from fornication, and each one of you to know how to use the body that belongs to him in a way that is holy and honourable, not giving way to selfish lust like the pagans who do not know God. He wants nobody at all ever to sin by taking advantage of a brother in these matters . . . We have been called by God to be holy, not to be immoral. In other words, anyone who objects is not objecting to a human authority, but to God, who gives you his Holy Spirit.'[30] 'Among you there must not be even a mention of fornication or impurity in any of its forms, or promiscuity: this would hardly become the saints! For you can be quite certain that nobody who actually indulges in fornication or impurity or promiscuity—which is worshipping a false god—can inherit anything of the kingdom of God. Do not let anyone deceive you with empty arguments: it is for this loose living that God's anger comes down on those who rebel against him. Make sure that you are not included with them. You were darkness once, but now you are light in the Lord; be like children of light, for the effects of the light are seen in complete goodness and right living and truth.'[31]

In addition, the Apostle points out the specifically Christian motive for practising chastity when he condemns the sin of fornication not only in the measure that this action is injurious to one's neighbour or to the social order but because the fornicator offends against Christ who has redeemed him with his blood and of whom he is a member, and against the Holy Spirit of whom he is the temple. 'You know, surely, that your bodies are members making up the body of Christ . . . All the other sins are committed outside the body; but to fornicate is to sin against your own property; you have been bought and paid for. That is why you should use your body for the glory of God.'[32]

The more the faithful appreciate the value of chastity and its necessary role in their lives as men and women, the better they will understand, by a kind of spiritual instinct, its moral requirements and counsels. In the same way they will know better how to accept and carry out, in a spirit of docility to the Church's teaching, what an upright conscience dictates in concrete cases.

12. The Apostle Saint Paul describes in vivid terms the painful interior conflict of the person enslaved to sin: the conflict between 'the law of his mind' and the 'law of sin which dwells in his members' and which holds him captive.[33] But man can achieve liberation from his 'body doomed to death' through the grace of Jesus Christ.[34] This grace is enjoyed by those who have been justified by it and whom 'the law of the spirit of life in Christ Jesus has set free from the law of sin and death'.[35] It is for this reason that the Apostle adjures them: 'That is why you must not let sin reign in your mortal bodies or command your obedience to bodily passions.'[36]

This liberation, which fits one to serve God in newness of life, does not however suppress the concupiscence deriving from original sin, nor the promptings to evil in this world, which is 'in the power of the evil one'.[37] This is why the Apostle exhorts the faithful to overcome temptations by the power of God[38] and to 'stand against the wiles of the devil'[39] by faith, watchful prayer[40] and an austerity of life that brings the body into subjection to the Spirit.[41]

Living the Christian life by following in the footsteps of Christ requires that everyone should 'deny himself and take up his cross daily',[42] sustained by the hope of reward, for 'if we have died with him, we shall also reign with him'.[43]

In accordance with these pressing exhortations, the faithful of the present time, and indeed today more than ever, must use the means which have always been recommended by the Church for living a chaste life. These means are: discipline of the sense and the mind, watchfulness and prudence in avoiding occasions of sin, the observance of modesty, moderation in recreation, wholesome pursuits, assiduous prayer and frequent reception of the Sacraments of Penance and the Eucharist. Young people especially should earnestly foster devotion to the Immaculate Mother of God, and take as examples the lives of the Saints and other faithful people, especially young ones, who excelled in the practice of chastity.

It is important in particular that everyone should have a high esteem for the virtue of chastity, its beauty and its power of attraction. This virtue increases the human person's dignity and enables him to love truly, disinterestedly, unselfishly and with respect for others.

13. It is up to the Bishops to instruct the faithful in the moral teaching concerning sexual morality, however great may be the difficulties in carrying out this work in the face of ideas and practices generally prevailing today. This traditional doctrine must be studied more deeply. It must be handed on in a way capable of properly enlightening the consciences of those confronted with new situations and it must be enriched with a discernment of all the elements that can truthfully and usefully be brought forward about the meaning and value of human sexuality. But the principles and norms of moral living reaffirmed in this Declaration must be faithfully held and taught. It will especially be necessary to bring the faithful to understand that the Church holds these principles not as old and inviolable superstitions, nor out of some Manichaean prejudice, as is often alleged, but rather because she knows with certainty that they are in complete harmony with the divine order of creation and with the spirit of Christ, and therefore also with human dignity.

It is likewise the Bishops' mission to see that a sound doctrine enlightened by faith and directed by the *Magisterium* of the Church is taught in Faculties of Theology and in Seminaries. Bishops must also ensure that confessors enlighten people's consciences and that catechetical instruction is given in perfect fidelity to Catholic doctrine.

It rests with the Bishops, the priests and their collaborators to alert the faithful against the erroneous opinions often expressed in books, reviews and public meetings.

Parents, in the first place, and also teachers of the young must endeavour to lead their children and their pupils, by way of a complete education, to the psychological, emotional and moral maturity befitting their age. They will therefore prudently give them information suited to their age; and they will assiduously form their wills in accordance with Christian morals, not only by advice but above all by the example of their own lives, relying on God's help, which they will obtain in prayer. They will likewise protect the young from the many dangers of which they are quite unaware.

Artists, writers and all those who use the means of social communication should exercise their profession in accordance with their Christian faith and with a clear awareness of the enormous influence which they can have. They should remember that 'the primacy of the objective moral order must be regarded as absolute by all',[44] and that it is wrong for them to give priority above it to any so-called aesthetic purpose, or to material advantage or to success. Whether it be a question of artistic or literary works, public entertainment or providing information, each individual in his or her own domain must show tact, discretion, moderation and a true sense of values. In this way, far from adding to the growing permissiveness of behaviour, each individual will contribute towards controlling it and even towards making the moral climate of society more wholesome.

All lay people, for their part, by virtue of their rights and duties in the work of the apostolate, should endeavour to act in the same way.

Finally, it is necessary to remind everyone of the words of the Second Vatican Council: 'This Holy Synod likewise affirms that children and young people have a right to be encouraged to weigh moral values with an upright conscience, and to embrace them by personal choice, to know and love God more adequately. Hence, it earnestly entreats all who exercise government over people or preside over the work of education to see that youth is never deprived of this sacred right.'[45]

At the Audience granted on 7 November 1975 to the undersigned Prefect of the Sacred Congregation for the Doctrine of the Faith, the Sovereign Pontiff by divine providence Pope Paul VI approved this Declaration 'On certain questions concerning sexual ethics', confirmed it and ordered its publication.

Given in Rome, at the Sacred Congregation for the Doctrine of the Faith, on 29 December 1975.

Franjo Card. Šeper
Prefect

Fr. Jérôme Hamer, OP
Titular Archbishop of Lorium
Secretary

Notes

1. Cf. Second Vatican Ecumenical Council, Constitution on the Church in the Modern World *Gaudium et Spes* 47: AAS 58 (1966) p. 1067.

2. Cf. Apostolic Constitution *Regimini Ecclesiae Universae* 29 (15 August 1967): AAS 59 (1967) p. 897.

3. *Gaudium et Spes* 16: AAS 58 (1966) p. 1037.

4. John 8:12.

5. Second Vatican Ecumenical Council *Declaration Dignitatis Humanae* 3: AAS 58 (1966) p. 931.

6. 1 Tim. 3:15.

7. *Dignitatis Humanae* 14: AAS 58 (1966) p. 940; see Pius XI, Encyclical Letter *Casti Connubii* 31 December 1930: AAS 22 (1930) pp. 579–580; Pius XII, Allocution of 2 November 1954: AAS 46 (1954) pp. 671–672; John XXIII, Encyclical Letter *Mater et Magistra* 15 May 1961: AAS 53 (1961) p. 457; Paul VI, Encyclical Letter *Humanae Vitae* 4, 25 July 1968: AAS 60 (1968) p. 483.

8. Cf. Second Vatican Ecumenical Council, Declaration *Graviasimum Educationis* 1, 8: AAS 58 (1966) pp. 729–730; 734–736. *Gaudium et Spes* 29, 60, 67: AAS 58 (1966) pp. 1048–1049, 1080–1081, 1088–1089.

9. *Gaudium et Spes* 51: AAS 58 (1966) pp. 1072.

10. *Ibid.*, see also 49: AAS 58 (1966), pp. 1069–1070.

11. *Ibid.*, 49, 50: AAS 58 (1966) pp. 1069–1072.

12. The present Declaration does not go into further detail regarding the norms of sexual life within marriage; these norms have been clearly taught in the Encyclical Letters *Casti Connubii* and *Humanae Vitae*.

13. See Matt. 19:4–6.

14. 1 Cor. 7:9.

15. See Eph. 5:25–32.

16. Sexual intercourse outside marriage is formally condemned: 1 Cor 5:1; 6:9; 7:2; 10:8; Eph. 5:5; 1 Tim. 1:10; Heb. 13:4; and with explicit reasons: 1 Cor. 6:12–20.

17. See Innocent IV, Letter *Sub catholica professione*, 6 March 1254, DS 835; Pius II, Propos. damn. in Ep. *Cum sicut accepimus*, 14 November 1459, DS 1367; Decrees of the Holy Office, 24 September 1665, DS 2045; 2 March 1679, DS 2148. Pius XI, Encyclical Letter *Casti Connubii*, 31 December 1930: AAS 22 (1930) pp. 558–559.

18. Rom. 1:24–27: 'That is why God left them to their filthy enjoyments and the practices with which they dishonour their own bodies, since they have given up divine truth for a lie and have worshipped and served creatures instead of the creator, who is blessed for ever. Amen! That is why God has abandoned them to degrading passions: why their women have turned from natural

intercourse to unnatural practices and why their menfolk have given up natural intercourse to be consumed with passion for each other, men doing shameless things with men and getting an appropriate reward for their perversion'. See also what Saint Paul says of masculorum concubitores in 1 Cor. 6:10; 1 Tim. 1:10.

19. See Leo IX, Letter *Ad splendidum nitentis*, in the year 1054: DS 687–688, Decree of the Holy Office, 2 March 1679: DS 2149; Pius XII, Allocutio 8 October 1953: AAS 45 (1953) pp. 667–678; 19 Maiy 1956: AAS 48 (1956) pp. 472–473.

20. *Gaudium et Spes* 51: AAS 58 (1966) p. 1072.

21. '. . . if sociological surveys are useful for better discovering the thought patterns of the people of a particular place, the anxieties and needs of those to whom we proclaim the word of God, and also the opposition made to it by modern reasoning through the widespread notion that outside science there exists no legitimate form of knowledge, still the conclusions drawn from such surveys could not of themselves constitute a determining criterion of truth', Paul VI, Apostolic Exhortation *Quinque iam anni*, 8 December 1970, AAS 63 (1971) p. 102.

22. Matt. 22:38, 40.

23. Matt. 19:16–19.

24. See note 17 and 19 above: Decree of the Holy Office, 18 March 1666, DS 2060; Paul VI, Encyclical Letter *Humanae Vitae* 13, 14: AAS 60 (1968) pp. 489–496.

25. 1 Sam. 16:7.

26. Paul VI, Encyclical Letter *Humanae Vitae* 29: AAS 60 (1968) p. 501.

27. See 1 Cor. 7:7, 34; Council of Trent, Session XXIV, can. 10: DS 1810; Second Vatican Council Constitution *Lumen Gentium* 42, 43, 44: AAS 57 (1965) pp. 47–51; Synod of Bishops, *De Sacerdotio Ministeriali*, part II, 4, b: AAS 63 (1971) pp. 915–916.

28. Matt. 5:28.

29. See Gal. 5:19–23; 1 Cor. 6:9–11.

30. 1 Thess. 4:3–8; See Col. 3:5–7; 1 Tim. 1:10.

31. Eph. 5:3–8; See 4:18–19.

32. 1 Cor. 6:15, 18–20.

33. See Rom. 7:23.

34. See Rom. 7:24–25.

35. See Rom. 8:2.

36. Rom. 6:12.

37. 1 John 5:19.

38. See 1 Cor. 10:13.

39. Eph. 6:11.

40. See Eph. 6:16, 18.

41. See 1 Cor. 9:27.

42. Luke 9:23.

43. 2 Tim. 2:11–12.

44. Second Vatican Ecumenical Council, Decree *Inter Mirifica*, 6: AAS 56 (1964) p. 147.

45. *Gravissimum Educationis* 1: AAS 58 (1966) p. 730.

Contributors

BARBARA HILKERT ANDOLSEN was born in the United States in 1946. She has a PhD in religion from Vanderbilt University and is assistant professor of religion at Rutgers University. She is the author of 'Agape in Feminist Ethics' *Journal of Religious Ethics* (Spring 1981) 69–83. Dr. Andolsen has been married for fifteen years and has two children.

SABINO ACQUAVIVA is Full Professor of Sociology at the University of Padua. He is a member of the scientific committee of the European Institute of Higher Studies at the University of Nice, and a Visiting Fellow of All Souls College, Oxford. His published works include, *Social Structure in Italy* (1976), *The Eclipse of the Sacred in Industrial Society* (1981) and *In principio era il corpo* (1983), as well as numerous articles in Reviews inside and outside Italy.

JOHN A. COLEMAN, SJ, a member of the board of editors of *Concilium*, was born in 1937 in San Francisco. He holds a doctorate in sociology from the University of California, Berkeley and has done advanced graduate studies in theology. He is currently Associate Professor of Religion and Society at the Graduate Theological Union, Berkeley, California. Among his books are: *Sociology: An Introduction* (1968); *The Evolution of Dutch Catholicism* (1978); *An American Strategic Theology* (1982).

GÉRARD FOUREZ, SJ, was born in 1937. He teaches in the department of human philosophy of science which he set up in the university faculties of Notre Dame de la Paix at Namur in Belgium. During the summer months he is visiting professor in the Graduate Division of the Department of Religious Education in La Salle College, Philadelphia, Pa (USA). He is a PhD in Physics (University of Maryland, USA) and a master of theology (S.T.M., Woodstock College, Md, USA). He is working especially on ethical questions connected with modern scientific technological society and its conflicts. His most recent publications include: *Choix éthiques et Conditionnement social* (1979), ET: *Liberation Ethics* (1982); *Foi pour les années 80* (1981); ET: *I Believe in God: What Do I Honestly Believe?* (Denville, N.J. 1982); *Les Sacrements réveillent la vie* (1982), ET: *Sacraments and Passages* (Notre Dame Ind. 1983). He has also written numerous articles, especially in *La Revue Nouvelle, La Revue Philosophique de Louvain, Lumen Vitae, New Blackfriars, Chicago Studies*, etc. He is a member of the editorial committee of *La Nouvelle Revue*.

JOHN H. GAGNON is presently Visiting Professor of Sociology at the Department of Sociology, University of Essex, England. He has done extensive research and writing in the area of sexuality. At the present time he is preparing a new book (with Professor William Simon) *Sexual Scripts and Sexual Conduct*.

RICHARD GRECCO teaches Christian ethics at the Toronto School of Theology. His doctoral dissertation was entitled, 'Theology of Compromise: A Study of Method in the Ethics of Charles E. Curran'.

SUSAN HANKS is a psychotherapist, researcher and educator practicing in Berkeley, CA. Born in 1947, she received a Bachelor's Degree from the University of Santa Clara in

1969, and completed her clinical training in psychiatric social work at Simmons College School of Social Work and the Massachusetts General Hospital in Boston, Mass. in 1972. Her interest in the field of domestic violence began a decade ago at Stanford University Medical Center where she studied the effects of alcohol use on violent behavior. This led to her recent creation of a research and treatment program for violent families at California School of Professional Psychology in Berkeley, CA. Because she views an individual's intra-psychic and interpersonal struggles as closely interwoven with his/her cultural and familial environment, she is active in community education and institutional and social policy change. She is grateful to her husband of 14 years and her 6 year old daughter for providing her with the opportunity to integrate abstract psychoanalytic, political, feminist concepts into everyday human relationships.

ANTONIO HORTELANO, CSsR, is a Redemptorist priest, born in 1921 in Irun (Spain). He gained a doctorate in theology from the Gregorian University in Rome and did psychological studies in Belgium and France. He is professor of moral theology in the Academia Alfonsiana (Rome), the Istituto Superior de Ciencias Morales (Madrid) and the Pontificia Universidad Bolivariana (Medellin, Colombia). Among his publications may be noted: *Yo, Tu: Communidad de amor* (1970) (Spanish, Italian, French, German); *La moral responsable* (1971) (Spanish, Italian, French, Portuguese); *La Iglesia del futuro* (1971) (Spanish, Italian, Portuguese); *El amor y la familia en las nuevas perspectivas cristianas* (1979) (Spanish, Italian); *EAS, Comunidades cristianas comprometidas* (1981); *Problemas actuales de moral* (1981) (4 vols).

JACQUES LAZURE, who was born in 1928, studied philosophy and theology at Ottawa (LPh and LTh), gained his MA in sociology at Notre Dame, and his PhD in sociology at Harvard. He did higher studies in sociology at Chicago and post-doctoral research at Berkeley. Since 1969 he has been teaching in the department of sociology at Quebec University, Montréal. He is particularly interested in the study of young people and has published three books on this subject: *La Jeunesse du Québec en révolution* (1970); *L'Asociété des jeunes Québécois* (1972); and *Le Jeune couple non marié* (1975).

RUDOLF SIEBERT was born in Frankfurt a.M. Germany in 1927. He studied at the Universities of Mainz and Münster, Germany, and at the Catholic University of America, Washington, D.C., USA. From 1962–65, he taught sociology, economics and theology at St. Agnes and Loyola College in Baltimore, Maryland. Since 1965, he has been Professor of Religion and Society in the Religion Department of Western Michigan University, Kalamazoo, Michigan. In the last three decades, he has concentrated on the philosophy of G. W. F. Hegel, the Frankfurt School of philosophy and sociology, and critical political theology. In 1977 he initiated and has since directed the international course on *The Future of Religion: Communicative Praxis-Communication Community* in the Inter-University Centre of Post-Graduate Studies in Dubrovnik, Yugoslavia. He is founder of *The Centre for Humanistic Future Studies* at Western Michigan University. His main works are: *From Critical Theory of Society to Theology of Communicative Praxis, Hegel's Philosophy of History: Theological, Humanistic, Scientific Elements, Hegel's Concept of Marriage and Family: Subjective Freedom, Horkheimer's Critical Sociology of Religion: The Relative and the Transcendent* (all by Washington, D.C.: University Press of America, 1979), etc. Rudolf and Margaret (+ 20 October 1978) Siebert are the parents of seven children.

XAVIER THÉVENOT, SDB, was born in 1938 in Saint-Dizier, France. He is a Salesian, and was ordained priest in 1968. He currently teaches moral theology at the Institut Catholique in Paris. He is a doctor of theology, and wrote his thesis on 'Homosexuality and Christian morality'. His writings include *Repères éthiques pour un monde nouveau* (1982), *Vie sexuelle et vie chretienne* (1982), a book for pre-adolescents, and *Les Péchés. Que peut-on en dire?* (1983).

CONCILIUM

CONCILIUM 1983

NEW RELIGIOUS MOVEMENTS

Edited by John Coleman and Gregory Baum   161

LITURGY: A CREATIVE TRADITION

Edited by Mary Collins and David Power   162

MARTYRDOM TODAY

Edited by Johannes-Baptist Metz and
Edward Schillebeeckx   163

CHURCH AND PEACE

Edited by Virgil Elizondo and Norbert Greinacher   164

INDIFFERENCE TO RELIGION

Edited by Claude Geffré and Jean-Pierre Jossua   165

THEOLOGY AND COSMOLOGY

Edited by David Tracy and Nicholas Lash   166

THE ECUMENICAL COUNCIL AND THE CHURCH CONSTITUTION

Edited by Peter Huizing and Knut Walf   167

MARY IN THE CHURCHES

Edited by Hans Küng and Jürgen Moltmann   168

JOB AND THE SILENCE OF GOD

Edited by Christian Duquoc and Casiano Floristán   169

TWENTY YEARS OF CONCILIUM— RETROSPECT AND PROSPECT

Edited by Edward Schillebeeckx, Paul Brand and
Anton Weiler   170

All back issues are still in print: available from bookshops (price £3.50) or direct
from the publisher (£3.85/US$7.45/Can$8.55 including postage and packing).

T. & T. CLARK LTD, 36 GEORGE STREET, EDINBURGH EH2 2LQ, SCOTLAND

X